CW00833544

A Parish Year

'Pastor Ignotus' writes a monthly column in *The Tablet*, the leading international Catholic weekly. His anonymity gives him freedom to write with honesty about the priestly life, but suffice it to say that he is a real priest, writing about real events that take place in a real parish, only known to readers as 'St Jude's'.

A Parish Year

Pastor Ignotus

Compiled by
Teresa de Bertodano

Illustrations by Pugh

Published in association with
The Tablet

CANTERBURY
PRESS
Norwich

© The Tablet 1998

First published in 1998 by The Canterbury Press Norwich
(a publishing imprint of Hymns Ancient & Modern Limited
a registered charity)
St Mary's Works, St Mary's Plain
Norwich, Norfolk, NR3 3BH

All rights reserved. No part of this publication which is copyright may be
reproduced, stored in a retrieval system, or transmitted, in any form or
by any means, electronic, mechanical, photocopying, recording, or otherwise, without the prior permission of the publisher.

British Library Cataloguing in Publication Data

A catalogue record for this book is available
from the British Library

ISBN 1-85311-208-9

Typeset by Rowland Phototypesetting, Bury St Edmunds, Suffolk
and printed in Great Britain by Biddles Ltd, Guildford and King's Lynn

May – First Impressions

In which the pastor accepts the parish of St Jude against his better judgment.

It all seems so long ago, but my first entrance into the parish was calamitous. It was one of those experiences that years later causes one to wake in the night and blush for shame. Could that really have been me?

As always, the whole thing began somewhere else and miles away. It was really an exercise in man-management where the skills are part natural and part supernatural, being a gift of the Holy Spirit which goes with episcopal ordination. The bishop had previously given me a job in education in the diocese, and a little urban ghetto parish which, looking back, was really a kind of pastoral hobby to keep me sane after the daily grind of the office.

It cannot be a mixed metaphor to say that the Holy Spirit is only too well aware of a man's Achilles heel. In any case, the bishop went directly for mine. He began, of course, with the hand on the arm and a murmured request for a quiet word. Clearly, I must be aware that the canon at St Jude's had been found dead in bed, life's fitful fever behind him and the New Testament open by his bedside.

Would I take St Jude's? For that is how it is done, consultations and wheeler-dealings apart.

Tactically, of course, one needs to catch one's victim off balance, and the bishop is an adept at this. It appears that he saw me as 'ruthless' and what he wanted was that a large parish which now had three assistants should be reduced to one priest and one assistant priest. I like to think of myself as compassionate: an ideas man, perhaps. But ruthless? Never!

What can one say? The bishop added a few simple words about my needing to be stretched and having obviously much more to give to the diocese than was at present the case. I had really only the obvious ploy left of asking for a few days to think it over.

The first thing was to go and look at the plant. The *Catholic Directory* told me that the church itself was over 100 years old. My heart fell. There was a large hospital; my heart fell further. I could never cope. Besides, there was a large comprehensive school and an upmarket primary school. I could hear the voice of Nobby Price from Shaw's *Major Barbara*: 'What price salvation nah?' And there were no less than seven old people's homes of various shades. Nothing for it but to go and look.

Calamity lay in wait. I walked round the church and presbytery from the outside. At the back, in among the broken plant-pots and the overflowing dustbins, there was a door which is etched in my memory. The door opened and one of the assistant priests emerged from the shadows. It was evident that I had been spotted from a neighbouring window.

'Is there anything I can do for you, Father?' he asked.

'Well, no, I was just looking!' I replied. It sounded lame and, on consideration, positively guilty.

Assistants, where their previous parish priest has been found dead in bed, are notoriously quick on the uptake when clerical visitors are noted on or near the premises. That this one was also what is known in the diocese as 'the Head Waiter', being next in line for a parish on the grounds of seniority of ordination, only compounded my embarrassment. I was caught and there was nothing I could do except smile nervously and admit that the bishop had sent me to case the joint. I refused an invitation to enter and said that I would call into the church to put the matter before the Lord.

Calamity, meanwhile, had moved nearer. The church was vast and echoing. A small red light in the distance indicated the presence of the Lord. I was glad he was near. In the narthex were two gentlemen in anoraks, large and composed. 'Are you the parish priest?' they asked, with heavy politeness.

I had an instinctive feeling I was being interrogated. How could I answer that? They wanted to know about a wedding for a certain McLean. I did not know.

'You are the parish priest, aren't you?' they insisted.

When I said 'Yes!', the die was cast.

I still did not know about the wedding and my interrogators were less than impressed. 'Not very co-operative, are you?' they remarked, as I showed them to the door in the gloom. It was only later, when I saw them mingling with the mourners at a funeral and patrolling the pavement opposite the church among the relatives from Mayo, that I realized they were Special Branch. So I had accepted the parish under pressure from the security forces. All right then, it must be the plan of a superior power that I should become the parish priest, but I felt I would never love this vast, echoing church or its people or its schools.

September

In which the pastor decides to improve his preaching and suffers a late-night phone call.

Early this month my assistant became quite excited when he read a report in one of the Sunday newspapers about the poor standard of many preachers' sermons. It confirmed in him the belief that the boring content or delivery of priests' homilies can be one of the main reasons why people cease coming regularly to Mass.

'What we need,' he shouted, thumping the breakfast table that particular Sunday, 'are homilies which challenge people to think. This means they should have punch, be short and pithy, contain a story and be relevant to the situations people are actually in.'

Never at my best first thing in the morning, I simply grunted and buried my head deeper in a newspaper of my own. I also refrained from asking what he would have made of a recent remark to me by our local bank manager, that homilies these days, with their emphasis on the readings, were too concerned with Christian behaviour and not enough with Catholic doctrine.

Shortly afterwards, I realized that my reticence had probably led my assistant to think I was not interested in what he said about homilies. This was both a pity and ironic, for only minutes before breakfast that morning I myself had scrapped a homily I had carefully prepared earlier in the week. Instead I was now hoping to deliver a different one that day and was desperately worried about the wisdom of so doing. My change of plan was because I wanted to use an incident in which I had recently been involved to illustrate what is meant by Christian commitment.

The previous night the telephone by my bed had rung loud and clear. Switching on the light and reaching for the receiver, I noticed that the clock said half-past eleven. I assumed it was either a sick call or an emergency and, for that reason, bit my tongue at the sound of a rude and aggressive voice at the other end. It turned out to be not in the least urgent, simply a parishioner demanding to know if I was the parish priest and then proceeding to harangue me about the thoughtless way her husband was treating her.

I quietly asked her if she was aware that it was now past 11.30 p.m. and that she was speaking in a rude manner, and went on to suggest that her story was not particularly urgent. In response, I was treated to a stream of verbal abuse.

'Surely,' she shouted down the phone, 'if you are a Catholic priest, that means you should be available to listen to anyone who rings you, whatever the time of day or night?'

I decided not to argue and about half an hour later, close to midnight, she completed her complaints.

After I had put the phone down, I found myself unable

to get back to sleep, plagued by conflicting emotions. I found myself annoyed, for example, because the parishioner clearly had not considered at all how I might feel. I wondered where the idea had come from that priests should be available, however trivial the matter might be, for 24 hours a day. Perhaps there should be a duty rota for priests, as in some parts of the United States. I asked myself whether the woman represented a type of Catholic who demanded too much of their priests and then became angry when they failed to live up to their expectations. Then I thought of all the people who lapse and blame their falling away from the faith on a priest with whom they have had a disagreement – the kind of outcome I had tried to avoid by listening to the parishioner's story.

Nevertheless, as I fell asleep, I felt ashamed at forgetting that I had been well advised many years before that to be at others' beck and call was part of what becoming a priest entailed. Why then was I complaining? I also knew I would not change my state for the world, whatever the disadvantages.

It was when I got up next morning that I had decided to substitute my prepared homily with one on the theme of Christian commitment, using the previous night's episode as a story, to illustrate the necessity for us all to be ready to respond to the needs of those who turn to us, whatever the inconvenience to ourselves. But when I heard my assistant at the breakfast table listing the qualities of a good homily, I had second thoughts. My new homily had few of the features he mentioned as being essential for preaching the Word.

When I got up from the breakfast table, therefore, I retrieved my old homily from the waste-paper basket. Before leaving the presbytery, I also suggested to my assistant that we might pursue this matter of improving our sermons by having weekly meetings together to prepare our homilies, compare notes and exchange ideas. He grinned at me and agreed.

So far we have had two useful meetings and, in the meantime, other clergy have now asked if they can join in. I only hope our homilies have improved. I fear mine still lack what my assistant insists on calling punch. Perhaps some good did after all come from that parishioner's late-night telephone call.

October

**In which the pastor and his assistant become
student chaplains and visit the sick.**

Ten days ago the bishop telephoned to say that my
assistant and I were required immediately to take on the
pastoral case of all Catholics at the local college of
technology. Apparently the college chaplain was in
hospital after a fall and had broken a hip, which meant he
would be out of action for the foreseeable future. I
attempted to persuade my assistant that we should regard
this new responsibility as a challenge, but he made it
abundantly clear that he was in no mood to have extra
work dressed up in euphemisms.

He already considered life at St Jude's sufficiently
challenging without the added task of dealing with
possibly hundreds of students, he said, and had
always maintained that most students fell into one of
two categories: either potential radicals and rioters, or
yah yah yuppies. When I quietly informed him that I
thought he was being somewhat prejudiced I was
treated to a withering glance, some muttered words
about some people still imagining they lived in the so-
called swinging Sixties, and the sound of the door

slamming behind him as he stormed out of the sitting-room.

Even so, the following day I thought a visit to the incapacitated chaplain might not only be charitable but also useful in enabling us to obtain more information about our new assignment. When I gingerly asked my assistant if he would care to accompany me to the hospital to cheer up the sick chaplain, to my surprise he immediately agreed.

Sitting by the hospital bed, I was reminded of the tutorials I received at university years ago. Instead of answering my questions about what was involved in work among students, the chaplain interrogated us about how we viewed our new role.

Paradoxically this approach completely disarmed my assistant; instead of feeling burdened with yet more work, he obviously felt flattered to be consulted and to have the opportunity to articulate his views, and rose to the occasion. He saw the task as fourfold. First, the chaplain was there to assist students to develop a dynamic relationship with God in prayer and through the sacraments, and to see this as crucial to the conduct of their lives; secondly, to encourage them to discover the relevance of the faith to their most important concerns and personal relationships; thirdly, to enable students to grow in their knowledge of the faith and to stretch their minds about it to the same extent as they were doing in secular subjects; and, finally, to assist them to integrate their faith with all they did, especially creative things, and so to accomplish something worthwhile in their lives after they had left college.

10

I hinted that this might be an over-ambitious programme and asked him how he would succeed even in engaging the interest of the students in the first place. He said that most of his ideas would be achieved through concentrating on character formation. He then proceeded to astonish both the chaplain and myself by pulling out of his pocket a battered paperback and reading out a quotation from the Jewish philosopher Martin Buber in support of his theory. 'Education worthy of the name,' he read, 'is essentially education of character. For the genuine educator does not merely consider individual functions of his pupil, as one intending to teach him only to know or to be capable of certain definite things; but his concern is always the person as a whole, both in the actuality in which he lives before you now and in his possibilities, what he can become.'

Just as remarkable was my assistant's further quotation from Buber that 'for educating character you do not need a moral genius, but you do need a man who is wholly alive and able to communicate himself directly to his fellow beings'. (I was instantly reminded of Irenaeus's remark that 'the glory of God is a human being fully alive'.) And all this, added my assistant, is achieved most effectively when done unconsciously.

What astounded me most at the hospital, however, was not how he had obviously already been thinking about chaplaincy work, but how the chaplain had been able to convert him from his previously hostile attitude towards students. And the key to this conversion to deep interest and involvement in their lives had been to give him a little affirmation.

11

So far the students have reacted splendidly to his presence among them and in turn have exercised what I can only consider a beneficial influence on him. They have induced him to give up smoking, to convert his car to lead-free petrol and use recycled paper whenever possible. They have also persuaded him to substitute an impressive-looking computer for his ancient typewriter. He solemnly assures me that all these things are important both for ecology and efficiency. Ominously, however, he also tells me that today's students are powerfully motivated by prospects of making money and talk endlessly about their careers. If he starts emulating them in those respects, I may have to remind him of what he said about the importance of character formation.

November

In which the pastor decides that the liturgy at St Jude's is a far cry from the splendours of Rome.

Few things seem to rouse Catholics to passion as much as liturgy. I discovered this many years ago, when I was assigned the job of acolyte at the head of a papal procession in St Peter's in Rome. Even now I can recall the excitement I felt as we lined up, and the shock that went through me when the curtains of the chapel where we had vested swung back, revealing the colossal length of the nave we had to process along. When row upon row of people crowding the basilica suddenly erupted with applause at the appearance of the Pope, and then simultaneously burst into singing, I distinctly remember being covered in goose-pimples.

What I was never able to decide, however, was whether or not this was liturgy. How, I asked myself, does one distinguish between liturgy and theatre, ceremonial and triumphalism, devotion and spectacle? In matters to do with worship, how should one judge between the claims of organs and guitars, plainchant and pop, Latin and the vernacular, solemnity and informality, not to mention silence and communal responses?

Today in our parish I am still asking these same questions. The only difference between now and then has to do with capacity: one cannot compare the apparently unlimited resources of Rome with the meagre potential of our parish. The combined warblings of Mary Dempster, Janet Walker, Pat Walsh, Joe Hennessy and Michael Reardon cannot vie with the Sistine Choir. The untidy servers at St Jude's, whose cassocks barely conceal jeans and trainers, are no match in appearance for the meticulously drilled and sprucely attired servers in our own cathedral, let alone St Peter's. Our aged master of ceremonies gallantly does his bit at folk Masses, but clearly has difficulty adjusting to changes in the Church since Vatican II. And what should we do about the old ladies who insist on reciting their rosaries aloud during Mass, the screaming babies and the young people who prefer to stand at the back of the church and will not sit down, no matter how often the ushers show them empty seats? Such thoughts came naturally to mind this month when the parish liturgical committee met to plan events for the first half of the approaching new liturgical year.

The first item on the agenda of the committee was Advent penitential services. These cause few problems, but discussion of Christmas midnight Mass preceded by carols is always a subject of contention. The leader of the Brownies was convinced that the miming of her little uniformed group to the singing of carols was what liturgists call participation. The organist called it a gimmick. The director of our latest sacramental

14

15

programme was eager for the parish catechists to form the offertory procession, and our organizer of the Rite of Christian Initiation of Adults thought it a good occasion for would-be converts to be involved in some way. In the meantime, the cantor, anxious not to be up-staged, complained that the carrying of the baby doll to the manger at the end of Mass was not in the rubrics.

At that point I found myself doubting whether this kind of discussion was what the recent meeting of bishops in Rome had in mind when they exhorted the laity 'to enter intensely into the life of their parishes'. Next, my assistant intervened to point out that the little girl chosen for the task of carrying the baby doll would see her mother a reader at midnight Mass, her father a special minister and her two brothers as servers, so she had to have a job otherwise it would appear like discrimination. It was of little help to my blood pressure that a retired naval lieutenant-commander on the committee then muttered that perhaps the Monopolies Commission might have something to say about one family exercising so much influence.

Pretending not to have heard his remark, we moved on to discuss next January and I invited the lieutenant commander (retd.) to liaise with the Anglican and Free Church leaders and organize some joint liturgical event for Christian Unity Week. This was possibly unkind of me, since I know he has difficulties with ecumenism and dislikes intensely the direction in which our bishops are encouraging us. I then braced myself for the annual cross-fire about what we should do liturgically in the weeks of

Ordinary Time leading up to Lent, when the committee would next meet.

Observing various members looking at their watches and anxious to go home, I decided to expedite proceedings. The only way I knew this could be done successfully, however, was to suggest that we simply followed the pattern of last year. In other words, we would try to please a different section of the congregation on successive Sundays; a process my assistant calls 'introducing confectionery Catholicism'.

I am not sure our committee's discussions would have met with the approval of liturgical experts. Obviously, too, our parish liturgy is a far cry from the kind I witnessed long ago in St Peter's. Even so, I like to think that what we lack in professionalism is compensated for by the sincerity of our worship. And what else ultimately matters?

December

In which the pastor discovers an angel in the loft and the Christmas crib proves a source of temptation.

The work on the crib has gone well, so far. An hour or two spent in planning has resulted in our having a framework of two-by-one timber all numbered in parts and linked with bolts and butterfly nuts. We now have the straw, the ox and the ass, the shepherds and angels, all carefully wrapped in newspaper to preserve the bright colours.

All this is carefully stored in the loft over and behind the high altar. There is a winding staircase up through what might appear as an extraneous round tower and there in the glory-hole is the most fantastic collection of bric-à-brac and memorabilia collected in over a century. Dust and debris are everywhere, stirred by the rat's foot only, year to year.

As a concession to modern technology, we installed a couple of electric light bulbs with a switch by the door and a two-way switch at the foot of the stairs. No one should have to undergo the stress inflicted on me by the assistant on my first visit up there. He carried the torch and I followed behind him since he knew what to expect. Inside the door and magnified by shaking beams stood a gigantic and monstrous figure.

When the light settled and I had decided not to fall through the trapdoor down into the transept, what emerged into the light was even more threatening. It is a contradiction to speak of a life-size angel carved in wood. Yet that is what faced me, dark brown with varnish and with the wing feathers picked out in tarnished gold leaf. The span of the outstretched wings would have been at least ten feet had it not been that one of the angel's wings had been hacked off and lay at his (?) feet. How else could they, so long ago have got her (?) into the loft up those winding stairs? The timber may have been valuable but there in the loft that malformed figure would have to remain. (There was also a nodding angel in the loft in addition to the winged one. Insert a coin and the head nods, even to this day, in lonely isolation.)

The Mother and Toddler group, who take their catechetics very seriously, were preparing the Advent wreath. Talk turned to 'cribs we have known' and there was a consensus that 'they don't make cribs like that nowadays'. Why not?

They had enough enthusiasm to mount a project. Of course, someone had to suggest running water. . . One mother went to the local garden centre and returned with a fair-sized garden pond in plastic. Husbands were dragooned, urged on by excited children, and the work was carried out during the early part of one never-to-be-forgotten night behind an enormous curtain which had once covered the crucifix in Passion week. An electric pump, operating on 12 volts for safety, moved the water round a lake and waterfall – and to our amazement it worked.

So great was the success of our crib that it was decided to leave it running until Presentation Day in early February. It so happened that a custom has arisen of throwing coins and, at times, folding money into the crib in appreciation.

Of course the word got out, and one afternoon when I switched on the lights in the church to read my Office there was a great scuttering from the crib. The local school had dispersed its juniors early because of the fog and some of the children had headed straight for the crib. They had loaded their pockets with the loot and to get at it had climbed into and over the life-size figures of Joseph and the ox and the ass.

Then came a terrified scream. One of the miscreants had pulled down the figure of a shepherd from the road on high which led from Bethlehem to the crib through our panorama, and was left behind, somewhat concussed. Scalp wounds bleed easily, and the figure of the shepherd was soon covered in blood. It was fortunate that the secretary had been a nurse. She dealt with the wounds competently and took the chastened looter home. I set about completing the dismantling of the crib, so ably begun.

January

In which a former altar boy causes trouble and
the pastor considers the difficulties of
youth-work.

January has been a gloomy month. There comes a time
when all seems lost. There was a telephone call from the
high school at three o'clock on a frosty, foggy afternoon
asking for help. The youth who was causing the
disturbance came from my parish, had been one of my
altar boys until he defected, and was now perched with
his boon companion on one or other of the pillars of the
main gates, jettisoning empty beer-cans and singing 'You'll
never walk alone'. In the nearby classroom the girls had
seized the opportunity to occupy ringside seats on all the
windows. The teacher had concentrated on damage
limitation and had got a message through to the front
office, to the head and finally to me.

How had things come to this pretty pass, and where had
we gone wrong? How far back should we go? There was
the break-up of the parents' marriage, the disappearance
of the mother, a care order, and the lodgement of the boy
with his grandparents, who were resolved to do their best.
He was blond, blue-eyed and had a charming smile which

would convince even the most hardened youth-worker of his repentance and firm purpose of amendment. We took him in tow, made an altar boy of him and relied on his grandparents to get him to the church on time, which they did.

But then they found a growing silence and the school noticed that he had returned to his bullying habits. It transpired that our best efforts had gone sour and wrong. After he had been involved in a street accident, the youth-worker, myself and the head had seen to it that he received adequate compensation. But then his mother had emerged from the shadows, and made clear that she intended to claim her share of the lump sum. From that day he went downhill.

More worry awaited me when our youth committee met to arrange the parish participation in the diocesan pilgrimage to Lourdes. It seems there was trouble last summer on two or three of these pilgrimages. The first signs came when a group of youths, girls and boys, travelling with the pilgrimage, were spotted commandeering a railway trolley to help in the transfer of their duty-free purchases. Later there was an emergency that entailed the evacuation of certain carriages at the rear of the train during the night. It turned out that a number of young people could not be easily roused, having begun their celebrations rather prematurely. Even then, a blind eye might have sufficed if a group of them had not emulated their footballing brethren by running through the town cheering for Manchester United, Leeds or Newcastle as the mood took them. Something would have to be done.

Recalling these embarrassments, the Lourdes committee proposed that an undertaking should be given by each and every person under 18 to abstain from all alcoholic liquors for the duration of the pilgrimage. This approach seemed to some to be unfair. Would the members of the committee themselves sign such a pledge?

On the other hand, these young people were expected to help with the transport of the sick: could reliance be placed on them if they had shown themselves irresponsible? The committee decided to depend on the principle which went back to Joseph Cardijn, the founder of the Young Christian Workers, and rely on the apostolate of like to like. Only a few known faces were involved and they would surely respond to peer pressure. There the matter rests for the moment.

The parish must work on. At every second door I call at, I find another victim of the raging flu which does not seem to yield to the current strain of anti-viral injection. There is no doubt that the elderly are at risk. It is clear that when troubles come, they come not as single spies, but in battalions.

As I return to the presbytery in the evening, coming along the convergent path is the good man who for three years has run the under-13, the under-14, and now the under-15 football teams. They have been models of efficiency, with teams chosen, transport arranged, and clean tackle always available. The principle is that a father will work hard for a football team as long as he has a son in it. And now he comes to tell me that the boy has met a girl, lost interest in football, and has been introduced to the drug subculture that runs round here. His father has

23

come to give me his resignation. All his good and honest work seems to have gone for nothing. It tears at the heartstrings to see a parent struggling, his honest effort and love apparently defeated.

We must close ranks; no patron or diocesan youth council can help us now. We are at the heart of the matter. Christ has redeemed our failures, our depression and even our flu. That was our inheritance at Christmas. We shall overcome.

February

In which the Pastor receives a surprising visitor and reflects on the pressures of the priesthood.

After a while you believe you can pick them. Early in the month my attention was called to a man in the church who had arrived shortly after the end of the first Sunday Mass. 'He asked about the time of the next Mass and he wants to see the priest,' I was told. I could see him from the sacristy. He looked slightly worn and crumpled. I knew he would try to touch me for cash and then be gone. I was about to have a quick bite of breakfast. 'Tell him to wait,' I said.

To my surprise he did. When I came back to the church, he was still there. Then, ten minutes before the main Mass, he appeared in the sacristy. I recognized the strategy: put the priest under pressure when he has little time to spare.

I reckon I am too soft a touch, but, strengthening my resolve to be firm, I led him through to the parish office. 'How can I help you?'

'Father, will you pray for me?' he said. 'I am not from these parts. I am visiting friends. My wife was killed in a motorway accident six weeks ago. I am not coping very

25

well. People have been kind, but I find it so hard.' He spoke quietly and with dignity. I promised him my prayers, shook his hand as he returned to the church, and, humbled, went to vest for Mass.

Afterwards, standing at the back, I saw Dorothy approaching. She had been to see me earlier in the week, tortured by some worry. Now she was smiling. 'Wonderful homily,' she declared. 'I am glad you understand at last.' Then she added with calm satisfaction, 'So you see, I *was* right.' I must confess that I was not sure of the connection she had made between our talk and the homily, but I was pleased if she had found comfort in it.

At that same Mass a movement had caught my eye. Teresa, an elderly parishioner, had slipped out during the Creed. By chance a friend of hers called a little later. I asked after Teresa. I wondered whether she had been feeling unwell.

Her friend seemed embarrassed. Then she looked straight at me and said: 'I might as well tell you. She is not ill, but she was upset by your homily. She went home, because she felt so hurt. She cried her eyes out and called you "a stupid man, who doesn't understand anything".' I could not guess the connection she had made either. (We sorted it out later.)

All in all, it had been quite a morning. And while the drama may have been exceptional, that kind of pressure is not.

It is commonly said that one of the hardest aspects of a priest's life is loneliness. That is true. It is not so much the matter of simply being on one's own. Many people have to endure that. It is rather the combination of this aloneness with this pressure. We have brought to us so many questions, worries, anxieties and tragedies on the one hand, so many joys and hopes on the other. It is a privilege. But there is also a weight of confidentiality that extends far beyond the seal of the confessional and often a sense of expectation that issues will be resolved. Nor is that the end of the matter.

Good pastoral care takes us into difficult territory. It heightens the pressure, because for us priests the distinction between the private and the professional is not too clear. People do not approach us out of need for cool professional guidance. That can be found elsewhere. They come to us to receive a care which is indeed professional, but which is also warmed by true friendship for them.

Here is a minefield. After all, we live in a society so preoccupied with sexuality that it seems largely to have lost sight of friendship. The scope for misunderstanding and disaster is obvious. But a Christian priesthood which has become too frightened to offer friendship and love might as well be extinct. We need a human touchstone, not to betray the secrets of others, but in order to share our own and so be sustained in our ministry.

Some find a way forward through the friendships they form with other priests. Many of us are blessed with a wide circle of friends. But kindred spirits in the priesthood and other dear friends are not necessarily close by when the darker clouds of pressure come down.

The old lesson is true: there must always be prayer as well.

Feeling the pressure earlier this month, as I have

described, and so a little downhearted, I decided to seek a prompt for prayer in St Paul's second letter to the Corinthians. I chose not to start at the beginning. I thought I would dip in anywhere. I picked on chapter four and read, 'Having this ministry by the mercy of God, we do not lose heart.' 'Oh, don't we?' I thought, and found myself smiling as I tried to pray.

March

In which the Pastor reflects on prayer, and Thomas and Sarah help their father to get a job.

It was an old and deeply experienced monk who convinced me that I was all wrong about prayer. I had grown up and been trained to believe, as I thought, that prayer was an end in itself, a goal to be worked for and attained and then enjoyed. But this is fundamentally wrong.

Prayer is not an end in itself. It is a means to an end, which is communication. When that communication takes place, the means fall away like the expendable parts of a rocket on its way to outer space. I was clinging on for dear life to the methods and means I had known and was left stuck up there in the outer atmosphere, most uncomfortably.

Now, the parish is riddled with all sorts of different methods of prayer, from the dedicated prayer group to the housebound invalid who says that if the pain is severe enough, she has only to close her eyes to be in the presence of God.

Then there is the Rosary Group. It meets in different

homes each week, recites five decades of the rosary, thinks about the mysteries of the Passion and the Resurrection, and the place of Mary in the scheme of things, then turns refreshed to the cup of tea and the biscuit which are such an essential part of the spiritual life of the typical ordinary parish.

And over in the schools the day begins and ends with prayer often gabbled and chanted in high-pitched tones like a mantra, but none the worse for that if, just for a moment, minds and hearts are lifted from the desks and the humdrum to the throne of God, even if only in supplication. Pain and hurt can be eased, and the injustices that can appear so horrendous to the young can be left at the feet of Christ for retribution.

There in the centre is the stillness of the hub of the ever-turning wheel, which is the tabernacle, and the permanent real presence of Christ. I am not the only one who can sit still and know that God is there. At odd moments throughout the day someone will drop in 'to pay a visit', as the jargon goes. We have written proof of that in the Intention Book which is a large ring-file with blank pages and a pencil or ballpoint pen attached.

This book, which is a record of prayers of petition and thanksgiving, could form the basis for this parish diary. Everything is there, from our local disasters on the roads and our worries about young people and drugs to lost jobs, redundancies and the repossession of homes. Many of our families are young and perforce mobile. This time last year we began to notice the forest of estate agents' signs – signals of the way the nature of the parish was changing.

At such times, prayers of anxiety and gratitude can be outlined in the Intention Book: as they were when the world of one young couple with two young children blew up in their faces. They had taken out a second mortgage to build an extension so that the children could have a room to play in. Now the husband had to move if he was to keep his job, the wife was unable at that stage to find a job in the new area, the children were bemoaning the loss of their friends; but worse – much worse – the house on which their prosperity was based had suddenly become a millstone round their necks, for buyers were few and prices had dropped. Their new home would cost them correspondingly less, but the saving on what they would have paid would not be sufficient to cover the gap between the price they could get for their present house and the double mortgage they had negotiated.

I sat on the low wall of the garden with Sarah – so-called, according to her father, because she laughed so much – and Thomas, conceived, born and brought to Christ in the sacraments under the protection of St Thomas of Canterbury. It seemed to me that now, if ever, we needed the miracle-working saint to help us. So we three – mother was in the house – decided that Thomas should ask his patron in a special way for help with Dad's job, the house and the new house they would require.

What happened left me shaking. We believed, the children and myself, that Thomas would help us. Why then was I thrown into confusion when Margaret, the mother of the family, flung open the door, telephone in hand, and called out: 'Yippee! Daddy says he's got the job and the promise of a deposit for the new house. Come and talk to him.'

To the children it was the most natural thing in the world. Where was my faith? Margaret came down the path to me. 'Thank God!' she said.

So St Thomas had intervened. I was there only because I had brought Holy Communion to the mother of three children a few doors further down. She was dying of cancer. Why could I not get up and go and cast out that devil? This kind could only be driven out by prayer, the Lord had said. Lord, I do have faith. Help the little faith I have.

April

In which the pastor goes shopping, and discovers differing views about the Easter liturgy.

My dream at this time of year is to achieve, in my ordinary humdrum parish, a genuinely participatory liturgy. Nothing less will do.

I was talking about this just the other day in the furnishing department of a large national store, as I waited for the curtains for the parish community centre to be brought up from the basement. Business was far from brisk, I noticed. No sign of a consumer-led recovery here.

The member of staff who served me was not one of my own parishioners, but belonged to a neighbouring parish. Nonetheless she had no difficulty in recognizing me and calling me 'Father', in spite of the anorak and working clothes I was wearing. We got to discussing the role of the parish choir and how discipline and dedication were essential.

I told her that I had invited a liturgical guru to be with us for the week before Holy Week and to stay with us until Easter Sunday morning. An aged monsignor, now gone to his reward, once remarked to me in all seriousness that the biggest single obstacle to participation in the liturgy was the dedicated musicians. Their sensitive ears find it hard to suffer the rest of us gladly. Our guru had his own stereophonic amplifier and he himself was endowed with galvanic energy. He kept our photocopier busy producing the scripts of plainchant which we practised night after night in what was intended to be a mood of prayerful anticipation.

Now, as I admitted in our continued conversation in the furnishing department, I am no musician. In fact, it began to appear that I would drive our genuine musician mad, with a cheerful attempt to come somewhere recognizably near the beautifully produced notes of his elegant scripts. Alas, a cheerful approach was not good enough; the only way to worship the source of all truth, beauty and goodness, he contended, was through perfection. Pushed to its ultimate conclusion, this began to seem like a fundamental difference between us on the nature of God. The God whom I was seeking to worship had sent his only begotten Son to share the human condition. Part of this condition must be cheerful acceptance of fellow human beings who can rise only to approximate rather than perfect pitch.

Half-way through our preparatory week I began to slip in at the back among the people of God as they practised, and was filled with admiration at their patience and humility. They were stopped in mid-flow, they were harangued and bullied, yet they loved it.

I was suffering from a bad conscience because I had been put off by our guru's opening remarks, when he pooh-poohed our concentration on the Easter Fire. We are very proud of our genuine bonfire in the piazza outside the church with its guard of Venture Scouts, bearing staves against hostile infiltration from the nearby pubs, and we had already planned a *pièce de résistance* of participatory enjoyment for the children of the parish and their parents. A cylinder of helium arrived, courtesy of the chemistry department of the local polytechnic (we paid for it, I hasten to add) and with it came the attachment required for filling hundreds of balloons. We tied on strings bearing the legend 'Christ is risen indeed' and the address of St Jude's Primary School and they are all filled and stored now under the protective covering of the old car port at the back of the presbytery.

Word of this has got out, as I found when the curtains arrived by the service lift and I prepared to take them down to the ground floor, where I was improperly parked at the rear of the building. This was preferential treatment, and there was a price to pay. Would I be so kind as to permit the good lady and her children to come to our Easter Fire and would they be allowed an Easter balloon to release, even though they were from another parish? Of course they would be welcome.

Now there you have the heart of the matter. This year we will be practised and we will sing as never before. We will move from the Blessing of the Oils through the Washing of the Feet until we come to the Celebration of the Passion. Then in our liturgy will come the explosion of the Easter Fire and the release of the Easter balloons into the night sky. Music has its part in all this, but our music, though enthusiastic, will never amount to much. We have done our best, but we are not a cathedral, and since the collapse from old age of our decrepit pipe organ we have had to make do with amazingly produced electronic noise. But no matter. We are involved, our children will be there in droves, and the balloons on Saturday night will soar with our hearts into the night sky.

May

In which the pastor and his assistant discuss
parish visiting and find that they are in for
some surprises.

When did a priest last visit your house? This was the
question I overheard a group of elderly ladies asking each
other after Mass, one Friday evening this month, as I was
closing the church doors. In the darkness of the porch
they did not see me locking up and perhaps I should have
joined in their discussion or at least have revealed my
identity. As it was, I quietly went away wondering for the
umpteenth time what to do about this vexed question of
parish visiting.

I must have looked preoccupied as I sat down to supper
that evening, for my secretary, who had just joined us,
asked me if I was feeling unwell and my assistant
remarked on my silence. Between the soup and the traditional Friday evening main course of haddock, I decided
to sound out my young assistant's views about priests
regularly visiting parishioners in their homes.

To start the discussion, I told him that I was wondering
whether we both might need to review how frequently we
visited the sick and elderly of St Jude's. I was quick to

point out that I was not talking about emergency occasions, when obviously one or other of us always turned out immediately and as a matter of course, but about regular and systematic visiting.

My assistant agreed that such parishioners were a priority, but reminded me that the last time I had worried about this, we had instituted our monthly afternoon Mass, preceded by confessions, precisely for them. He went on to point out that for these Masses transport was provided for all the sick who then not only received Holy Communion but were also anointed; afterwards they were provided with tea in the parish hall and so had a regular opportunity to meet and speak, not only with their friends and other parishioners, but with the priests. He added that the sick and elderly were visited in their homes virtually every week by eucharistic ministers who kept us informed of their condition.

In an effort to change the direction of the conversation, we talked about how, several years previously, the plight of young wives in our parish of St Jude was particularly noted. Many of these, with husbands at work, had felt trapped in their homes during the day, because they could not leave their young children behind when they wanted to go out shopping or visiting friends.

To solve this problem, crèches at strategic points in the parish had been organized. This had meant, of course, that subsequently more young wives and mothers, in addition to those who already went out to work, were away from home in the mornings. My assistant confirmed that ever since he had come to St Jude's, any parishioner found at home in the morning was likely to be an unemployed man, who often felt embarrassed at the priest discovering him in bed, babysitting, or doing the housework and cooking.

We both agreed that late afternoons and early evenings had also become inconvenient times for visiting. In the past, it may have been very true that priests visiting parishioners in their homes at such times would often have found whole families sitting around the meal table. Nowadays, however, a visiting priest frequently found families not together but eating from individual tables, facing not one another but the television set, unable or unwilling to give much attention to anybody else in the group, let alone a visitor from outside.

By now the conversation with my assistant had become desultory, if not depressing. I had not improved matters by telling him of the remark I had over-heard, uttered outside the church earlier in the evening by the elderly ladies. When my secretary heard it, she became so upset that I feared she would do herself an injury.

Have those ladies ever considered, she demanded, that in the so-called good old days you priests never had to sit on countless diocesan commissions and parish committees, and so had the time to visit? Have they measured the time you have both had to devote recently to the parish-based First Holy Communion and Confirmation programmes, whereas instruction for the sacraments in the old days was given in school? Are they aware, she almost shouted, of how many engaged couples you prepare for marriage, the baptisms and funerals you perform, the hours you spend counselling people with problems, to say nothing of the number of Masses they expect you to say?

Before finally flouncing out of the room, she added that it was time parishioners realized their own responsibility for visiting, as part of their Christian vocation to evangelize. In her view, she said, priests should hold surgeries like doctors, at regular times, and not allow parishioners to harbour expectations about home visits from priests that could not be fulfilled.

Both my assistant and I fell silent. I suspect we both felt that neither the elderly ladies outside church nor my secretary were completely right. There is surely somewhere a happy medium between the two extremes.

June

In which the pastor discovers the telephone to be a mixed blessing.

The telephone bill has arrived. Is this a moment of truth? Not particularly, as far as I am concerned. And for two reasons. In the first place, the total is comfortably less than £200. I know there are some priests who would be apoplectic if the amount was even half that size. They haunt their assistants as soon as they go near a phone. I have no time for that. I do not mean to encourage wastefulness. That would be foolish. But I share the view of a priest friend of mine who once described the phone as a pastoral aid. That is the second reason for my unconcern. It is important to be economical, but as a priest I cannot be too anxious about a telephone bill.

The telephone, of course, is a mixed blessing. It can bring entertainment; it can be a form of penance; it can be a vital link to those in need; and it can be a delightful contact with friends who lift the spirits. This month it has been all those things for me.

It rang early in the month and a voice said, 'Good evening, Father. It is Father, isn't it?'

I told him it was and wondered what was coming next.

'Do you think I could come and see you and have a chat? In fact, I'm not of your faith, Father, but I respect all religions. Geoffrey is my minister. He came round to talk to me for two hours the other day.'

I sent up a silent prayer of thanksgiving for Geoffrey, whom I know and like and see regularly at our fraternals. He is obviously endowed with great patience.

'Actually, Father,' my caller went on, 'I phoned you before, but, as there was no reply, I wrote to the Pope.'

So there you have it, in the view of this good man: should Pastor Ignotus be unavailable, you can always try Pastor Supremus. Our conversation rambled on. I have not heard from him again. But after the news of his letter to the Pope, other items seemed rather an anticlimax.

The phone can also become a form of penance. There are days when it seems to be ringing all the time, but that is not what I have in mind. I am thinking rather of those situations when you are trying to help someone who rings again and again and again. You want to give your support, but you cannot live on the telephone. There are other parishioners with other needs.

John was beaten frequently by his stepfather when he was young. The bruises healed long ago, but his opinion of himself was severely damaged. He blames himself. In his eyes the brutality was his fault. He is no good. He comes to see me regularly and we try to restore his self-esteem. The process has been slow and difficult. I believe, however, that real progress has been made. But our gains are fragile, for he is vulnerable. The slightest knock can send him tumbling down again. When he is on the slide, he will phone me and talk on. I try to give him time, but

43

I also try to judge what time is appropriate. It is not easy. For if his mood is dark and he senses I am bringing the conversation to an end, he will very swiftly register my indication of limits as withdrawal from him and rejection. Sometimes, I suspect, he prolongs our conversation until I have to bring it to a close. By doing so, I have then confirmed his worst suspicions: that he is no good, worthless.

It is difficult to deal with such a problem alone. Confidentiality very properly forbids my talking about it. I have misgivings about introducing it into this diary, but do so because I suspect that there are many others trying to cope with similar situations.

Some parishioners have got to know that John calls round and takes up a fair amount of my time, but they are unaware of the true nature of his problem. They are ready to supply solutions. 'I wouldn't stand for it,' they say. 'He's being manipulative,' or, 'He's just seeking attention.' Would that it were so simple.

It is not only a matter of long, draining conversations. There can also be a series of calls, four or five within two hours. At certain times he needs constant reassurance, and doubts or tries to undermine every attempt I make to supply it. It can be very stressful.

The temptation is to stop answering when he rings. I am glad that I resisted it the other Sunday afternoon. The last in the series was not from John at all, but from a nursing home in the parish: Barbara at a great age was at last close to death and I was being called to be with her. Here was the link with someone in need.

I have left till last the sheer pleasure of being able to

speak to friends on the telephone. I thankfully acknowledge that. Even in times of stress these calls can make me laugh, lift my spirits and keep me faithful.

July

In which the pastor celebrates a marriage but fails to distinguish himself.

Here at St Jude's we are now well into what I call the marriage season. Our records show that from April to September there are on average at least three weddings a month in our parish church, and the number is increasing every year. This, however, has very little to do with religion. It has much more to do with the fact that St Jude's is the only church in the city which possesses a lawn. For the purpose of wedding photographs and nowadays, more often than not, home videos, nothing can beat pictures of the happy couple, surrounded by their relatives and friends, which show them grouped on the lawn with St Jude's in the background.

To prevent our church becoming for all and sundry simply a fashionable place in which to be married, we have tried to restrict weddings at St Jude's either to parishioners or to those who have family connections in the parish. Even so, it is amazing how quickly people can discover some long-lost second or even third cousin living in the parish, in order to justify their application to be married here. It is not unknown, too, for applicants to claim that their great-grandparents were married at St Jude's and use that as a reason.

My assistant has a whole repertoire of reactions when couples endeavour to convince him that if they are not married at St Jude's their great-great-aunt, who they are sure lives within the parish boundaries, will be most upset. If he also suspects that the Catholic party may not have set foot in a church for years, he often solemnly enquires whether it was wise to have already booked the florist, the organist and the professional singer, not to mention the photographer and the reception room at the nearby posh hotel, before coming to see the priest.

By contrast he considers me quite soft and cowardly when faced with couples from outside the parish who provide the flimsiest of reasons for wanting to be married at St Jude's. Last week, therefore, he had a field day, telling me it served me right, when at the wedding of one such couple everything one dreads on such occasions actually happened.

I am used by now to brides being late at the church on their wedding day and, indeed, once or twice in my ministry they have failed to appear at all. I am accustomed to bridegrooms forgetting the wedding ring or simply through nerves losing their voice. It is a relatively minor matter, too, if the organist plays the wrong hymn or the reader reads the wrong reading. What I have never previously experienced is a series of disasters from beginning to end of a marriage ceremony.

First, the bride arrived very late, her chauffeur having been stopped by the police for speeding on the way to the church. Then, as she processed down the church, her hooped wedding dress got out of control. Clearly she had never practised walking in a hooped dress before and so, with each step she took, the hoop rose higher in the air.

Her father, accompanying her down the aisle, suffered from what I call Dr Johnson's disease – that is, the need to touch the end of each row of pews as he passed them. (Apparently Dr Johnson when walking in the country could never pass a fence without touching every post.) The final humiliation for the bride as she made her entry was the slow slipping sideways off her head of her wedding veil. What with a bride attempting to control her dress and veil and a father preoccupied with touching pews, they made a sorry sight.

I managed to begin the ceremony without batting an eyelid, anxious only to reassure the bride.

When, however, at the exchange of vows, her future partner promptly fainted on the floor and had to be picked up and revived with a glass of water by his best man, I began to wonder what could happen next. By the time of the nuptial blessing, the bride's mother had clearly had enough and burst into tears.

The following day, when I sounded out my assistant as to whether he thought I should visit the two families who seemed to be so accident-prone and offer them some comfort, he surprised me by saying that perhaps I should offer them instead a profuse apology. When I asked him what I had done that required forgiveness, he went on to suggest that I should first obtain a copy of the video of the wedding. In his opinion, he said, the camera had possibly captured one of my finest hours at St Jude's and certainly one worth keeping on tape in the parish archives.

Did you realize, he asked, that throughout the entire wedding ceremony a tear in your cassock revealed a cricket sweater underneath, that a tie of the local cricket club was hanging out of one of your pockets, and that your white socks and slacks protruding below your cassock were bound to be seen on the video? In short, from your appearance your impatience to be off to a cricket match was obvious to all. If you do not believe me, he said, you should remember that the camera never lies. I stood rebuked.

August

**In which the pastor takes a holiday and
reflects on the joys and sorrows of celibacy.**

I was lucky enough to go on holiday this month. I had
been looking forward to it all summer. As I stood outside
church after Mass the day before I left, one of the parish
comedians came up to me. There was the beginning of a
smile in his eye.

'You're very fashionable these days,' he remarked.

I looked at him blankly. 'Come on,' I said, 'what is it
now?'

'Haven't you noticed?' he went on. 'Celibacy has
become smart.'

How could I fail to have noticed? It has been difficult to
miss the various newspaper articles and television
programmes which have discussed the matter. So I left for
my holiday the following day, fashionably celibate, but,
thanks to the comedian, musing on an irony, for a holiday
is often the time for me when being celibate is most
difficult, my sense of aloneness most acute. While I was
away, I tried to tease out the question.

It struck me at once that, though I am celibate, it is not
in fact in any fashionable sense. The fashionably celibate

seem to be those who fear AIDS, those who have been wounded by unhappy love affairs, and workaholics who have no desire to waste their energy on sex. These reasons for celibacy may have some merit, but they do not apply to me. Terrible as AIDS is, it is not this which has prompted me to celibacy; I am not the survivor of a tragic love affair; nor am I celibate in order to be freer to work harder. Why am I celibate? What led me to this?

Before I began training for the priesthood, while I was still at school, I can remember a priest whom I admired asking me what I thought the hardest part of a priest's life would be. I answered, 'celibacy'. He agreed. But, although I was able to give that answer and accepted celibacy not merely as a necessary undertaking in order to be ordained, but positively, deliberately and willingly, I know now that I was too young and inexperienced to appreciate the commitment I was making. Does that invalidate my young decision? I think not. Were the Church's discipline to change and my personal circumstances in due course to alter as well, I would be happy to be a married priest, but, as it is, I remain celibate positively, deliberately and willingly, and moreover gladly, without reluctance. As the years pass, my appreciation of celibacy grows. It does not become any easier – in some ways it is harder – but I understand it better and value it more. Why? I thought again about the fashionably celibate.

Whatever the reason for their celibacy – whether the fear of illness, personal hurt or the demands of work – they seem to be in flight from relationships. I am not. And I would guess that all those of us who are unfashionably celibate would say the same.

Our Gospel calls us to relationship, to love God and to love others. Any Christian way of life that denied that call would stand self-condemned. If I found I could only be celibate by avoiding loving, I would abandon it instantly. But it does not make such demands on me. On the contrary, it requires me to attend to my love for God and for those I meet. The two loves are inseparable. And I would say that I have been lucky.

Friends have been my great good fortune. If I have been at all able to live my celibate life with a certain warmth and ease and approachability, then the credit is largely theirs. But it is not easy. We live in a society which scarcely understands friendship. It tends to assume that close, personal relationships must be genital as well as affective. That cynicism is unjust; and it is also inhibiting. Being celibate is not easy.

Nor is it tidy. After all these years, loving faithfully in a celibate way is not something I have solved. I have to work at it. There can be times of real strain. Friendships have a dynamism. They change. I change. I need to be sensitive to what is in others and what is in me. But one lesson I have learnt; faithful celibate loving cannot be discovered from books. It is to be found in the lived experience that holds together a longing for union with God and a delight in our friends.

Many years ago I realized whom I would have wished to marry had I not been a priest. That secure knowledge has been a source of great strength to me. At the same time I long harboured the worry that my love for her to some degree compromised my love for God. My head could reconcile these loves, but my heart was torn. They seemed to be rivals.

One evening during my holiday, sitting alone on a hillside and wondering about these things, my heart suddenly grasped at last what my mind already knew. I felt overwhelmed with love both for God and for her. I knew without doubt that there was no rivalry. It was a moment of grace.

September

In which Joe joins the seminary and the pastor considers the shortage of vocations.

This month our parish had the great joy of sending a young man to the seminary to train as a priest. Joe is only the second from St Jude's to try his vocation to the priesthood in the past ten years. Indeed, so unusual these days is such an event that we celebrated a special Mass on his last Sunday among us; a Mass which included prayers that he might persevere. A few days later I drove Joe to the seminary.

In the weeks which had preceded the bishop's acceptance of Joe for training, I little knew that his wish to become a priest would raise all sorts of questions in the parish, many of which may never be satisfactorily answered. The very fact that Joe is a very gifted person and, after graduating from college, chose the priesthood rather than other walks of life amazed more than a few parishioners, including some of the most practising and devout.

Since Joe is very attractive to the opposite sex and at one stage had a girlfriend of long standing, I could understand why one or two young women in the parish were less than delighted at the idea of his becoming a priest. On the other hand, I was rather taken aback when several parents expressed relief to me that it was not one of their sons going off to the seminary. This was particularly noticeable, incidentally, among the more well-to-do parishioners.

Whereas I could more readily accept that parents whose sons had opted for secular careers in banking, insurance, electronic engineering, the civil service and so on, were to some degree puzzled by Joe's behaviour, I was disturbed by the reaction of others. One mother, for example, whose three sons had each sought employment in the fields of nursing, teaching and social work respectively, went so far as to ask me why Joe had not chosen a more useful way of life. A father of two small boys was very fervent in his hope that neither of them would ever ultimately become a priest, so long as the pay, conditions of work, holidays and prospects on retirement for priests were so archaic.

After becoming aware of how much fear and even hostility could be aroused among parents by the idea of their sons becoming priests, I naturally began to wonder whether the decline in numbers for the priesthood would ever be halted, let alone reversed.

Inevitably I began to question whether all of us, including young men who in the past might have considered the priesthood, were now intoxicated by the counter-attractions of a materialist and consumer society. Was the shortage of vocations also partly due to other forms of community service being more readily available nowadays? Was the lack of parental encouragement somehow due to their desire to see their sons married and themselves becoming grandparents? To what extent was the decline in numbers related to the possible decline in social status of the priesthood? Perhaps most important of all, I began to worry how many young men might have been put off trying their vocation by seeing the kind of witness to Christ given by priests, including myself. On the car journey to the seminary, I decided to ask Joe what he made of all this.

Surprisingly, he swept aside as superficial all the questions parishioners had posed about the usefulness of the priesthood and how he might be better employed. He was sad that so many seemed not to understand the nature of a vocation and how at its core it was a mystery of love as great as that which can exist between a man and woman. He confessed to being hurt when friends implied that he was wasting his life by becoming a priest. How can time spent with God ever be wasted, he asked.

He quickly recovered his sense of humour at the thought of the lack of social status he would experience as a priest; he tended to think that would be a bonus and something to cherish. He also laughed enormously and with relish at the prospect of not being able to make a fortune as a priest; he was delighted never to be able to be a yuppie.

Instead, Joe preferred to go straight to the heart of celibacy. He was of the view that celibacy was certainly going to be hard, but that it was something positive to be embraced, not something to be endured in a stoic fashion or as a discipline. Furthermore, it was up to him in prayer to ensure that his relationship with God remained vital and alive. Just as friendships with others were like fences that needed to be kept in good repair, he said, quoting the poet Robert Frost, so it was in his relationship with God.

Then he went on to compare commitment to God in priesthood to fidelity within marriage. But in the same way couples genuinely in love can never totally describe their reasons for wanting to get married, neither could he fully explain his wish to become a priest.

He did manage, however, to silence me when I asked him whether he thought priests, including myself, were witnessing sufficiently to Christ to attract others into the priesthood by example. He muttered something to the effect that priests varied as much as did human faces, but that I had had an influence in his decision to try his vocation. I suddenly felt very small.

October

In which the pastor hears some home truths from his assistant and helps an unexpected visitor.

My assistant is of the opinion that parish councils are the invention either of the Jesuits or of Opus Dei. Who else, he frequently asks, could have devised a system of enabling parishioners to voice their views, yet cunningly deny them the means of taking action? How else, he enquires, do I account for the fact that parish councils are only advisory bodies, with executive authority residing solely with the parish priest? Where else, he insists, are people either elected, selected or chosen at whim to sit on a council and then, if they start questioning matters, told that the Code of Canon Law does not even require that they exist?

Small wonder I braced myself in readiness for the October meeting of our parish council at St Jude's. Dealing at such meetings with difficult parishioners is one thing; living in the presbytery at such times with a sceptical assistant is another. I have to tread warily, for he is expert at recalling the number of occasions in the past when I have mounted my own hobby horse and complained about the pressures of priestly life. It is then that he will remind me of how often I become annoyed at the frequency of the phone ringing, the door bell sounding and the umpteenth 'gentleman of the road' demanding a mug of tea and sandwiches, not to mention money to help him on his way. If in a truly mischievous mood, my assistant will mention when I have groaned at the prospect of attending meetings of countless committees in the parish – all seemingly invented since Vatican II – such as those concerned with finance, liturgy, catechetics and adult education, justice and peace, and social events, to mention just a few. He is also adept at remembering how often I have deplored the enormously high expectations so many of the laity have in regard to their priests and the demands they are capable of making of them. As an exit line and before I hurl a book at his head, he has been known to quote me as saying in a rash moment that it was a pity priests were not allowed to marry, if only because wives would never put up with our present lifestyle.

Oddly, it is invariably in October, and prompted by the impish utterances of my otherwise kind-natured assistant, that I am liable to fall victim to pessimism concerning the pressures of parish life. This past month then, by way of circumventing such a possibility, I invited a group of sixth formers from our local Catholic comprehensive to meet the assistant and myself so that we could hear their views on priesthood.

By way of opening the discussion, I asked them if they considered priests so be people working under pressure and whether this might account for so many priests suffering migraines, ulcers, chronic backaches, heart diseases and so on. They thought this a possibility but were of the opinion that the pressures experienced by priests were not any greater that those experienced by many of their parents. Similarly, they spoke of others, not only priests, who felt their days to be full of endless 'shoulds', 'musts', 'oughts' and 'have-tos', allowing little time for reflection, beauty, culture and travel.

I found this all very salutary until they proceeded to insist that a priest should be a man of prayer, a good preacher, a liturgist, an adult educator, a home visitor, an administrator, a spiritual director, a counsellor, a committee person, a possible chaplain to a school, hospital or prison and a builder of churches. For good measure they added that he should keep abreast of modern theology and be available at all times for his parishioners. How one person could possibly be expected to be all these things was never explained, for it was at that memorable moment, as I was about to explode, that there was a loud knocking at the front door.

When I opened the door there stood a middle-aged man in tears, shaking all over. He said straightaway that he was not a Catholic but that he needed to talk to a priest. I invited him in to the presbytery and sat him down, whereupon he immediately told me that his wife had left him two days previously, taking their children with her. He felt he ought to pray, but had not done so for over 20 years and in any case had forgotten how. He said he knew that he needed God's help, so had come to me, a priest, for advice.

I therefore endeavoured to make him feel at ease and welcome, my assistant made him a cup of tea and, when the sixth formers had gone, we allowed him to ventilate his anger and pain. Above all, we attempted to alleviate his loneliness. It was when my assistant and I finally succeeded in bringing a measure of comfort and calm to our unexpected visitor, that it occurred to me that in the discussion with the sixth formers nothing had been said about the joys and sense of fulfilment to be found in priesthood.

I therefore remembered the blessings of priesthood when we celebrated our patronal feast of St Jude on the 28th; an occasion when both my assistant and I resolved to stop our complaining about so many things in our daily parish life. We have not forgotten, however, that St Jude is the patron saint of hopeless causes.

November

In which the Sisters take on a pastoral role and the pastor hears more home truths.

Some time ago, following lively discussions within the parish council and after an approach had been made to various religious orders, two nuns arrived at St Jude's to begin work on an experimental basis as pastoral assistants. This month the parish had a visit from the mother general of their order, who came to see for herself how her Sisters were faring. We were all fearful she might withdraw them, but we need not have worried.

When I and my assistant had initially spoken to the parish council about employing full-time pastoral assistants, we were adamant that they should be recognized and treated as co-workers with the clergy. We further asked that if it were feasible pastoral assistants should be female, in order that they might bring their own particular insights to pastoral care. It was then that the parish council hit on the idea of inviting two nuns to join us at St Jude's.

I vividly remember the Sisters' major concern over lunch at the presbytery on their first day. They had never previously worked in a parish and so naturally wanted to know what was expected of them. Attempting to be utterly pragmatic, I told them their first task was to knock on people's doors and learn to drink gallons of tea. If they were invited into a house, I said that at least during an initial visit they were not to ask the occupants when was the last time they went to Mass, and whether or not they sent their children to a Catholic school.

It was at this point that the telephone rang and I had to leave the room. As I was returning I could not help overhearing my assistant holding forth. Describing me as 'the old man', he was telling the Sisters that I was not completely mad and that I was a typical example of a parish priest who was doctrinally conservative, but pastorally quite innovative. He went on to say that at first he too had thought some of my ideas a bit weird, but in time they had proved okay. And then, just as I was flattering myself that this was quite an accolade, coming from my assistant, he ended by telling the Sisters that at least they did not have to live with me, which was a quite different kettle of fish.

Behaving as though I had heard nothing of this, I nevertheless thought it prudent on my return to explain to the Sisters why I had given them the advice that I had. I told them that whenever they were invited into a home their first task was to try and ascertain what chiefly preoccupied the people who lived there. It might be the fact that they had recently suffered a bereavement or were recovering from an illness, that a baby was shortly to be born to one of the family, that the young couple they were visiting were obviously living together but were unmarried, that the father of a family was ashamed of being unemployed, that a member of the household was an alcoholic, or that the young one of another was a truant from school. As I observed the Sisters' eyes widening with wonder at what they had let themselves in for, I emphasized that the important thing was to be sensitive to the situation of the family one was visiting and, above all, to develop the faculty of listening. I told them that only then would they know at what point and how to speak of matters of faith.

Somewhat reassured but still apprehensive about what lay in store for them, the Sisters then left the presbytery in the car provided for them by the parish. Before lunch they had already visited the flat bought for them by the parish on a large housing estate and where they would live with the overhead costs borne by the parish on their behalf.

The Sisters took me at my word. They have visited countless homes in the parish, particularly those of the sick and elderly. They have alerted my assistant and myself whenever anyone has needed anointing or any housebound person has requested confession. On one memorable occasion, in the middle of the night, they even washed and laid out a dead woman while I comforted her distraught husband downstairs. They have organized a crèche for young mothers trapped in their homes with toddlers during the day, and have established a drop-in centre for those who want to discuss a problem over a cup of tea. They are currently arranging regular social gatherings in the parish hall for retired parishioners. Apparently days of prayer and retreats for overworked parishioners are next on their list. And they tell me that they have only just begun.

I told their mother general that it was difficult to remember what life was like at St Jude's before the Sisters came. In a manner I thought a shade over the top my assistant informed her that if she were to try to remove the Sisters, he would lead parishioners in protest demonstrations. She replied that she found it equally hard to believe the transformation that had taken place in the Sisters. Her major concern now was whether they could ever be expected to live again in a traditional religious community, so happy had they become. I myself am convinced that the advent of the Sisters as pastoral assistants is the best thing that has happened in years at St Jude's.

December

In which the nativity play proves a mixed blessing and the pastor celebrates Mass for people with disabilities.

It never fails. There is always a moment in the nativity play in the primary school when the throat tightens and one is raised, rather than reduced, almost to tears. There is no predicting which child, which character in God's presentation of himself on earth will trigger it, although I have yet to be moved by the Archangel Gabriel. This year it was the leader of the Roman soldiers, a tough 11-year-old altar server with a rasping voice who is a promising striker in his football team. Roman soldiers are normally played for laughs: bullying, bumptious villains whose actors throw themselves into the part. This year their forte was the stamping walk, a spine-jarring thump at each step, down the hall, then back to the stage. But at the end he led them in their silver-painted cardboard helmets and short red cloaks without that drama, and they were simply another group of children walking up centre stage; he took off his helmet and genuflected to the infant Jesus, and as his company of brutal soldiers copied him the hall was still and silent. There was no explaining it. Mary and

Joseph knew their parts perfectly, she the taller by a distracting couple of inches; the shepherds were strong on awe; the kings were the most naturally dignified I have ever seen. But this year, in this school, the privilege of being the catalyst of devotion belonged to that boy.

The Mary of the infants department was chubby, and had her own special gift for stillness. Towards the end her self-consciousness and concentration had worn off, and while the rest of her class sang 'Away in a Manger' she gazed into space. A teacher with a guitar looked anguished. Was it because of Mary's indifference to convention, or because one group of six-year-olds was singing roughly one bar behind another, neither group showing any sign of distress or conflict?

But these questions disappeared once the real crisis, worthy of Joyce Grenfell herself, began. It occurred during the most tedious part of any nativity play, the children of every nation sequence. This year they attempted a dance of uncertain ethnic origin, but vigorous, and the paper costume of one little girl began to disintegrate as she dervished away in front of the crib. In a moment, devotion to the Baby Jesus changed into desolation. Turning her back on the tableau of the Holy Family, she faced us as if to make a speech, pressed the remnants of paper to her hips, and burst into tears. The headmistress was on the stage at once and knelt in front of the child. What happened then could not be seen, but when the headmistress got up in less than a minute and left the stage with a peremptory signal to the accompanist, both morale and costume had been repaired sufficiently for the child to resume her dance. All credit to the efficiency and

experience of the headmistress, but it was the sort of incident that made me think of a guardian angel of nativity plays; I have never been to one, however trite or tatty, which failed to rise above its human ingredients.

There was almost too much angelic power in the Advent Mass for people with handicaps. How can one describe the sound and appearance and behaviour of over a hundred disabled people in a small church without belittling their human dignity? Only aversion and embarrassment is shameful there; but admitting to these reactions does not necessarily banish them. 'Don't worry,' said one of the organizers, the same powerful demand that the angel made of Joseph, and as the Mass proceeded it seemed that those with disabilities, their families and helpers were in charge. The readings and bidding prayers, the offertory procession, the serving, everything was accomplished by co-operation, slow, trusting, unbeatable. Not even in the schools was there so strong a sense of identification with Jesus' birthday; each time it was mentioned, the people responded with murmurs and cries. There were indeed uncomfortable moments, but these came not from the proximity of people with handicaps but from our habit of ignoring them. No amount of talk about their place and importance in the Church could provide a fraction of the impact of their Mass.

Was there a time when adults performed nativity plays? All we seem to have is carol-singing. But for us who share the church building with members of other denominations, this is a key activity which forces us to overcome divisions: not the great principles of the theologians, but the trickier, or at least more immediate, problems of hymn books and organists and mince pies. Peace, said the angels, and in spite of all our fears it came.

January

In which the pastor goes to court and finds that there is a great deal wrong with the system.

A parishioner wrongly accused of assault asked me to attend the magistrate's court with him in order to provide a character reference. We had to sit in the public gallery for a couple of hours before his case was called. I had not been inside a court room for some years, and I was surprised at how distressing I found the whole experience. The majority of those brought before the magistrate were young, disadvantaged and clearly inadequate. I suspect some were unable to follow the proceedings for the simple reason that the language and the accents to which they had to listen in the court were so different from what they were accustomed to in the street.

A pathetic-looking 18-year-old girl stood shivering in the dock. The court was told she was a drug addict and was also undergoing tests for cancer. She had been brought back to court for failing to pay the fines which were imposed upon her when she had been convicted for 'loitering' a few weeks previously. My parishioner, who was sitting beside me in the public gallery, whispered in my ear: 'You know what that means – it's a court euphemism for "soliciting".' The magistrate, a pompous-looking fellow, was told that she was unemployed and was at the time living in a hostel.

There was a short pause in the proceedings as the magistrate consulted some papers on his desk. He then looked up and, peering over his glasses, spoke in a voice which lacked any hint of compassion: 'You've two weeks to pay up or else you'll come back here and face a custodial sentence. Do you understand there can be no excuses next time?'

The young girl gave a feeble nod of her head in his direction. 'Yes Sir,' she said.

As she was being escorted out of the dock she turned towards the magistrate and said, 'Please Sir, can you tell me how much I have to pay?'

He looked at the clerk who consulted a pile of papers on his desk and then replied: 'You owe the court £340.'

By this time I was feeling so angry and frustrated at what I had witnessed that I wanted to stand up and shout at the magistrate. 'You pompous old fool! Where do you think this young girl will get that amount of money in two weeks? Don't you understand you are sending her out to walk the streets again?' It was only the thought that I would have to apologize to him after such an outburst or face the possibility of being charged with contempt of court that made me at the time exercise self-restraint. The magistrate seemed to be more concerned with keeping his books straight and following the letter of the law than caring for the well-being of this vulnerable youngster. The fact that she was likely to return to prostitution again to pay her fine did not seem to bother him. In fairness to him, however, I suppose that if you are dealing with this sort of case on a daily basis it is easy to become hardened to the human factor. He might also have argued in his own defence that his task was to apply the law and not to act as a social worker.

The plight of that young girl has haunted me ever since. I feel bad that I did not step in and offer to pay her fine: I also feel ashamed that I did not have the courage to register my protest in some way or other, at the time. On reflection, though, I suspect that the way in which she was dealt with by this particular magistrate's court may not be uncommon. The attitude of individual magistrates is, of course, extremely important, but the real fault seems to lie with the legal system itself. In the parish we have a number of lay and stipendiary magistrates who are kind and compassionate people, but I fear they may well find themselves locked within a process which does not give them the scope to deal with the vulnerable youngsters who frequently appear before them.

In the course of my parish ministry I have met a number of prostitutes who have been quite open about their work. Many of them explained to me that the reason why they took to the streets in the first place was simply to make ends meet. They had been abandoned by their partner and were unable to provide for the children on what they could earn in a shop or receive from Social Security. But the young girl I saw in the magistrate's court was one of a growing number of young people who are taking to prostitution in order to feed their drug habits.

I mentioned this to a local doctor, a specialist in drug

addiction, who told me that one of his own sons spent –
in less than six months – over £50,000 on sniffing cocaine.
He raised the money by leaving home and working as a
rent boy. He has now broken the habit, the doctor told me
with relief, and is working in a clinic helping other young
addicts to do the same.

Although I spent many years studying moral theology in
the seminary, I frequently find myself ill-prepared to cope
with such pastoral tragedies and my human instinct tells
me that the people caught up in them need a fatherly
embrace rather than a moral lecture.

February

In which the bishop pays a visit and the pastor's assistant decides that bishops are not so bad.

The month of February will be etched in the memory of many of us at St Jude's for a long time. It was the month when, out of the blue, there arrived a letter from the bishop informing us that he intended to come and celebrate Mass in the parish before the month was out.

This news came as a blow to those responsible for the cooking, who fretted that, because it was Lent, they would not be able to lay on an impressive spread for him. It was the signal for a certain amount of panic from the sacristan, the altar servers, the choirmaster and organist; all worried about not having sufficient time to rehearse an event they clearly regarded as the equivalent of grand opera. The parish council suddenly became concerned with protocol and argued at length as to whether these days they were expected to genuflect and kiss the bishop's ring, or simply shake his hand in a manner implying that they knew their rights as part of the People of God.

The mother superior of the local convent, on the other hand, showed no uncertainty as to what she and her

community would do. I was informed that she and her Sisters would be occupying the front two benches at the Mass celebrated by the bishop. Most ordinary parishioners were simply bemused by the news and wondered why the bishop had suddenly taken it into his head to come to say Mass at St Jude's at all. The only person who considered that there must be an ulterior motive to the visit was my assistant. When, therefore, he asked facetiously one morning at the breakfast table whether I thought the bishop would arrive in an anorak or full pontificals, I took it as an opportunity to try to allay his suspicions. I also particularly wanted to assure him that on the whole bishops should not be underestimated.

I told him that bishops come in all shapes and sizes, different colours and dress, and with an amazing variety of manner and background. This, I went on, is only befitting in a Church that is universal and which embraces all races and cultures. Those of England and Wales, however, are usually immediately recognizable – apart from one, or at most two, maverick exceptions which the Holy Spirit somehow managed to slip through, when the eye of Rome must have been looking elsewhere. Generally speaking, I continued, even if most of our bishops cannot be classified as high-flown intellectuals, they usually show signs of being holy men. When he looked sceptical, I tartly reminded him that anyone could be clever, but it was quite difficult to become wise. Did he really want intellectuals the equivalent of a former Bishop of Durham in our midst, I asked. Thinking that I might have sounded a shade uncharitable to one of our separated brethren, I tried another tack and assured him that virtually all of the bishops (with one amazing exception who is unique in any case) tend also to be moderate in their opinions and conscientious in their duties as shepherds (in some cases to the point of being workaholics). For good measure I described many of them as at least shrewd and often wily in their judgments.

By this time my young assistant was getting restless, so I decided to terminate my lecture by telling him that bishops also have to be able to take flak, make unpleasant decisions, discern the truth from flattery, and be able to suffer fools gladly. When he intervened to ask how they were appointed, I told him that was neither here nor there, but a mystery and not something he should worry his head about.

As probably befits a fiery and zealous young man, who often reminds me of myself when I was his age, he greeted my litany of episcopal qualities with a scoff, making it sound as though he considered I was sycophantic in my views. He suggested that in my assessment I had left out a quality required of all bishops in their duty of governing, teaching and sanctifying a diocese, namely their need to understand that real day-to-day power in the Church did not lie with themselves, whatever Vatican II might have said, but with parish priests. And with that cryptic remark he stormed off. I later learnt that he had proceeded to startle the devout few of the parish who come to daily Mass, by telling them that perhaps we should all regard the bishop's forthcoming visit as a particularly heavy Lenten penance.

In the event the visit passed off remarkably smoothly. The bishop arrived at the wheel of a modest-sized car, wearing a black suit, clerical collar and simple pectoral cross. He was neither casual nor pompous and seemed to have an uncanny knack of knowing precisely what kinds of thing different people needed, as well as expected, him to do and say. At Mass and in his manner towards the altar boys, the choir and folk group he came across as someone who put people at their ease; with the congregation, including the nuns sitting half-way down the church (the front pews were occupied by people with handicaps), he was very much a caring shepherd. And when he told us all that the cause of his visit was his decision to promote my assistant as a parish priest, I suspect he finally made it, even in his eyes, as a father in God.

March

In which a new assistant arrives and the pastor finds him surprisingly conservative.

I had been warned by other parish priests that sooner or later I would encounter the phenomenon. It was all very well, they said, for me to pooh-pooh the idea, think they were exaggerating and pulling my leg. This month I know they were in earnest. They had been telling me about an unaccountable new breed of young priest; a type that many of us thought had disappeared at Vatican II.

Even so, when my new assistant arrived in the parish, I received a shock. What particularly startled me was the cast of the new man's mind, his view of priesthood, not least in relation to the laity, and the virtually complete absorption he had in events that occur only on the sanctuary. He is the complete antithesis of my last assistant, trained over a decade ago, who was something of a firebrand and constantly talked about our need as priests to show solidarity with the deprived and oppressed. He had little time for ceremonial, was rarely seen in a clerical collar and was happiest campaigning for better housing and more jobs for the poor of the parish.

His replacement, by contrast, is utterly conservative (with a little 'c') in every sense of the word.

Like parishioners in most places, the ones here at St Jude's give every newly arrived priest about three months' grace before they reveal how they feel about him. Nevertheless, it is obvious that the majority are this time having a hard time keeping their mouths shut. Outside the church after Mass on Sundays I have problems exercising custody of the eyes in regard to those parishioners endeavouring to offer me, albeit tacitly, their sympathy with looks of condolence.

In the meantime, what I most fear is division within the parish. A minority of parishioners, for example, are particularly taken with his penchant for ceremonial, for antique vestments, and for long-forgotten priestly privilege; they share his voiced dislike of Sisters functioning as pastoral assistants, women readers, special ministers, Folk masses and every conceivable type of parish committee. No one yet, including me, has seen him out of his full-length cassock and I confess that in a moment of uncharity I have wondered whether he has a biretta at the ready for Easter.

The remarkable thing to me is that, unlike those who are rallying to his cause, he is just 30, so he would not even remember pre-Vatican II times. If he obtained his views in the seminary, what does this mean, I wonder? When my fellow parish priests, whom I consulted on the golf course, started grinning at my predicament I decided it was time to act.

After much thought, I called an extraordinary meeting of the parish council, ostensibly to discuss the forthcoming

Easter ceremonies, but in reality to create a forum in which parishioners would be free both to advise and to ask me and my assistant any questions they liked. I even contemplated contacting my former assistant and getting him to issue a three-line whip to some of his former radical cronies, but in the event resisted the temptation.

In any case, it proved unnecessary. The meeting turned out to be the most robust and best attended I can ever remember. Clearly the bulk of parishioners had got the message that I felt under siege and needed rescuing. Sometimes I am amazed at parishioners' kindness.

On the suddenly vexed question of women readers at the Easter ceremonies, I thought that Dan Jones, a former classics teacher and organizer of the readers' rota, was superb. It is true he has often in the past driven me to distraction with his insistence on using editions of the Bible most accurate in their translations from the Greek, but that evening I forgot such things. When my assistant spoke of St Paul having written of women knowing their place, Dan, no champion of the cause of feminism, was nevertheless swift to quote St Paul's acknowledgement of his indebtedness to 'our sister Phoebe, a deaconess of the church at Cenchreae' and to 'Prisca and Aquila, my fellow-workers . . . who risked their own necks to save my life' (Romans 16:1, 3). The meeting voted overwhelmingly in favour of women readers remaining.

When we went on to discuss the music for Easter, my assistant proposed the banishment of Folk music – for ever.

The usually quiet and unassuming Mary Kemp, our extremely talented parish organist, threatened to resign if such a proposal were passed. That caused many to pause and reconsider. After all, Mary would not say such a thing unless strongly provoked. The minority also remembered that she is virtually indispensable for our monthly Latin Mass, when the choir take their lead from her with their Gregorian chant. A passionate intervention from the leader of our thriving youth club in support of Mary settled it, and the meeting came to a rapid close.

Over supper that evening my new assistant generously admitted that he had a lot still to learn, particularly about other people's feelings. I fear, however, there will still be occasional squalls ahead of us. In case the next matter of controversy should be about priestly vestments, I have taken the precaution of removing any fiddle-back chasubles and other pre-Vatican II vestments from the sacristy.

April

In which the pastor is committed to Christian unity but finds that there are practical problems.

'What did you think of that?' Margaret asked Jenny, when they met on the Bank Holiday after our United Service on Good Friday. Margaret is a devoted, but not notably ecumenically-minded, parishioner, Jenny an Anglican friend. They had both been at the service.

'All right,' was the reply. 'We went, we prayed, we sang, we had a cup of tea, and we came away.'

'Not much evidence of impact there, Father,' Margaret observed with an amused shake of the head, as she relayed the exchange to me later. Perhaps not. But our commitment to unity must not falter.

I had had a hand in preparing the service, inspired by what I had heard of groups walking to Walsingham at this time.

I have never been myself, but I have been told that the Holy Week ceremonies there are impressive. In particular those who have carried crosses for about a hundred miles over different routes speak of the power of the moment when the different pilgrimages converge on the shrine and see each other for the first time. From various directions they come together. We tried to follow this example in a humble way.

Our local Methodist church is set next to an attractive park close to the centre of the town. Our council of Churches agreed that we should gather there for an evening service of repentance and prayer, song and praise on Good Friday. And it was indeed a touching moment as we converged across the parkland – Anglicans, Catholics and United Reformed – three separate processions coming closer together to be welcomed by our Methodist friends into their church for united prayer.

No doubt there were occasions like that all over the country. I hope so, because our quest for unity seems to be in disarray at the moment.

In the parish where I worked before, efforts at co–operation and common purpose were well developed. The Week of Prayer for Christian Unity was not at odds with the rest of the year, but observed among the churches in a variety of imaginative ways as a celebration of all that we did together regularly. It was a time of thanksgiving for the real, even if imperfect, communion we had already achieved. It involved as well considerable understanding of our diverse theological and spiritual traditions.

Matters are different here, more confused. I am always made most welcome by other clergy and invited to play a full part, which I try to do; there is a great deal of evangelical warmth; but there seems to be little knowledge of the Catholic position. Without ill-will the understanding I had known before is lacking. The situation is complicated further for me by the fact that this parish is so large territorially that I belong to two different clergy fraternals. That creates problems, problems of time, political problems and problems of purpose. Let me try to explain.

The problem with time, of course, is simple: there is not enough of it. And although I try to attend all the meetings, quite often I miss, because of other engagements which have to take precedence: funerals, pastoral crises, diocesan meetings.

What I have called political problems can be illustrated most obviously from my particular circumstances. One fraternal devised a plan this year for contacting all the homes in our joint parishes with a leaflet announcing our Holy Week and Easter services. I pointed out that this Catholic parish extended further than theirs. Would we be covering its entire area? John Moore's face fell. He is an Anglican and had been the prime instigator of the scheme. 'Oh wait a minute,' he said. 'That would mean the times of my services being circulated in homes in other Anglican parishes. It would look as though I were poaching.'

We had to drop that plan and settle for a joint advertisement in the local newspaper.

And the problems of purpose: my colleagues seem to be for ever forming extra plans, meetings and marches and groups, as if there were not enough to do already. And so I am aware of a conflict within myself: the desire to identify with and support these other ministers, on the one hand, while, on the other, feeling the schemes they design are an added burden when I already have as much to do as I can manage.

These scattered thoughts can supply no neat conclusions. And they barely scratch the surface of what may be about to happen.

'I am totally opposed to the ordination of women,' one local Anglo-Catholic vicar remarked to me last November, 'but I have no desire whatsoever to become a Roman Catholic.' He never comes to any fraternal. Down the road another Catholic-minded priest is reported to have told his congregation: 'We'll all be Roman Catholics in five years' time.'

Christian unity was never going to be easy, a matter of realizing one day with delight that somehow we had all been right all along. There was always going to be a dying if we were to rise as one. And now suddenly in the midst of Eastertide, Calvary seems more daunting than ever.

May

In which the pastor helps a young parishioner whose fiancé is suffering from AIDS

I was not in the least prepared when after Mass one Saturday evening this month a young parishioner appeared in the sacristy in distress. When I called her by name and asked if there was anything I could do for her, she promptly burst into tears.

It was then that she informed me that, two weeks previously, she had accompanied her fiancé to the sexually transmitted diseases clinic of a hospital in a nearby town to be tested for AIDS antibodies. That morning he had received the result and had been found not only to be carrying the virus but to have developed AIDS itself. What could they do about it, she cried?

During all my years as a parish priest I have come across so many people with tragedies in their lives that I had begun to suspect that I was becoming immune to shock. My greatest fear was that I might also by now have become hardened, even cynical. Would there come a time, I had wondered more than once lately, when I would find myself unable to muster the proper compassion in a given pastoral situation? But this was a vain worry; her anguish upset me enormously.

Here before me was an attractive young woman whom I knew to be the pride and joy of her parents, both devout and practising Catholics. Jenny had grown from an intelligent child at the parish school and then the Catholic comprehensive into a vivacious and popular student at university. Her two older brothers were once altar servers and members of the parish youth club. I could scarcely take in what she was desperately trying to tell me. This kind of thing doesn't happen to decent people, I found myself stupidly thinking.

I took Jenny into the presbytery, sat her down and telephoned her parents to tell them she was with me and that they were not to worry. I then asked my assistant to make us a cup of tea and allowed Jenny to take her time before speaking again.

When she did speak, she told me that she had first met her fiancé at university and both of them had been attracted to each other. They were studying the same subject, attended the same lectures, and discovered they shared similar interests. She had brought him home several times and he had accompanied her to Mass.

At the end of their second year it was clear to all in the parish who knew them that they were in love and it came as no surprise when they announced their engagement. Soon afterwards, however, Jenny began to notice a change in her fiancé's personality and behaviour. Instead of being interested in his studies he appeared listless and unable to concentrate. He was now almost always tired, constantly complained of his glands being swollen and of having night sweats, was unusually forgetful, and then began to lose a great deal of weight. What Jenny did not know was that small purple-coloured lesions, later diagnosed as Kaposi's sarcoma, had also begun appearing on his feet.

Jenny demanded to know what was worrying him. It was then that he confessed that on an extended trip abroad, between leaving school and coming to university, he had had several casual sexual relationships. He now feared that, as a result, he had acquired AIDS.

This news, together with its later confirmation at the clinic, devastated Jenny. She is now angry because she feels her fiancé has been given a death sentence and her hopes of marrying him have been blighted. Being intelligent and informed she has read a great deal of literature about AIDS. She knows there is no proven cure or vaccine against the virus. She frets about the possibility of her fiancé going on to develop the more horrendous symptoms sometimes associated with this dreadful syndrome. She worries about how much time they have left together, but has become more anxious that they concentrate on making the most of every moment. Her great fear is that her fiancé will be treated as a social outcast, especially as it was very difficult at first to persuade her parents to overcome their initial hostile reactions to the news.

It was with a heavy heart, then, that I drove Jenny home that Saturday evening. It was clear to me that in the coming weeks and months ahead, Jenny and her fiancé would need all the love and support St Jude's parish could give them. Fortunately there is a trained AIDS counsellor in our deanery to whom I turned and who immediately provided both Jenny and her fiancé with professional assistance and moral support. The AIDS help-line in the city also informed us precisely where practical help could be obtained. The hardest task, however, remains: educating the parish to cast out its prejudices and fears on the subject of AIDS. In my view, only when that is accomplished will St Jude's be able to help Jenny and her fiancé effectively as a Christian community.

June

**In which parishioners 'shop around' for
Sunday Mass and the pastor's assistant
becomes even more conservative.**

I presume that it is a universal practice in every large
city these days for there to be a fair amount of what is
called 'shopping around' when it comes to going to Mass
on Sundays. In the city, where St Jude's is simply one
parish among many others, we have long been
accustomed to knowing that certain parishioners keep
their Sunday obligation elsewhere other than in their
home parish.

Until now I have not thought too much about this,
simply assuming it was largely due to more people today
owning their own cars and being more mobile. I was also
more concerned that they should go to Mass than
bothered about which church they attended. Lately,
however, I have had reason to revise my opinions.

The arrival of my new assistant has meant that I have
been forced to consider what happens to a congregation
when a priest is moved and his replacement decides to
change the way the liturgy is celebrated. I have also found
myself asking whether we are becoming prone to what I

call the Anglican tendency for congregations to be spoken of as 'high', 'broad' or 'low' and in our case 'traditional' or 'progressive'.

Mass at the cathedral, for example, is especially popular on account of it boasting a fine organist, trained choir and all the facilities for a liturgy celebrated with dignity if not a certain amount of panache. I envy the ability to inculcate in worshippers a sense of awe, often absent in the liturgy elsewhere. I suspect, however, that people seeking anonymity, opportunity for private devotions during Mass, and anxious not to be roped into any parish activities also gravitate there.

St Michael's, on the other hand, on the outskirts of town, is a magnet for Catholics anxious to see the Church more committed to justice, peace and ecology; you name the cause, whether it be Greenpeace, Amnesty International or CND, and you can be sure it will feature on the church notice board and be mentioned in the Sunday bidding prayers. The parish priest and the regular worshippers at St Michael's have probably been on more rallies and marches than I have had hot dinners.

Our neighbouring parish of St Agatha's is quite the opposite; its parish priest is deeply involved in the charismatic renewal, eschews mention of social issues and draws a quite different kind of congregation from around the city. Healing services and prayer meetings, which include speaking in tongues and the uttering of prophecies, are the order of the day.

Here at St Jude's we have hitherto tended to steer a middle road, our only innovation being a regular youth Mass which attracts large numbers of the young. This is sometimes a Folk Mass but basically it is a celebration influenced by the liturgy and music of Taizé. Since the arrival of my new assistant, however, I have had to assure the young people that the youth Mass will continue.

It is true that, even before my assistant's arrival, I used from time to time to ask myself how much people's attendance at Mass was determined by the way a particular priest said Mass, the length of his homily and so on, and how much by their understanding of the sacrifice of the Mass. In the last few weeks this has become no longer an academic question. What I now fear is that the preconciliar niceties which my new assistant brings to the Masses he celebrates will divide rather than unite, the parish community, if only because they are already tending to attract a particular clientele, not to say élite.

It is difficult for example to explain to young people in particular why he prefers to give Holy Communion to people when they are kneeling, refuses to give it in the hand or under both kinds and will not exchange the sign of peace even with altar servers. So far I have ignored questions from others as to why he insists on inserting prayers that used to be in the old rite but are not in the new. What bothers me is that clearly there is a growing conflict in some people's minds between nostalgia for the past and the legitimate place of the laity in worship.

My problem is exacerbated by the fact that my assistant is no rabble-rouser but a soft-spoken and doggedly determined soul. The only time so far that I have actually had occasion to rebuke him was when he insisted on speaking loudly of heretics and hell at an ecumenical function we held just after Easter. He has also crossed swords with the formidable mother superior of the local convent; an event which unfortunately has only deepened his distrust of the part women play in the Church. Rumour has it that her parting shot to him was the remark that he was better suited to the Greek orthodox enclave on Mount Athos where all things female are forbidden.

June for me at St Jude's, then, has been a bothersome month, relieved only by the joy of a beautiful summer. There have even been times when I have envied the laity who can enjoy the luxury of being able to 'shop around' for Mass on Sundays. My rather ignoble motive for doing so at the moment would be the search for a bit of peace.

July

In which the pastor celebrates Mass for the sick, and Molly helps the children to understand death.

Once a month for the past seven years here at St Jude's an afternoon Mass for the sick and housebound of our parish has been celebrated. At this Mass anyone who is in any physical or mental pain has the opportunity to receive the Sacrament of the Sick, in other words to be anointed, and to receive Holy Communion.

An army of volunteers provides transport for those who would otherwise have difficulty in attending these Masses. Such is the popularity of these occasions that, to passers-by, the church at such times must often resemble the casualty department of a hospital, with people being taken inside on stretchers, in wheelchairs or on crutches.

The music and singing for these Masses are provided by the children from our parish primary school. At an early age they are thereby encouraged both to be of service to those in need and to come to terms, in as natural a way as possible, with old age, suffering and death.

By now the children have long appreciated that the Sacrament of the Sick is not something confined to the dying. Often, too, they have observed the comfort and relief provided by anointing. They have also frequently become firm friends with the sick and elderly. One such person whom they particularly love is Molly.

As a child Molly grew up in an orphanage, having been abandoned by her mother and never having known her father. After leaving school at 14, she soon became an unmarried mother and her child was taken into care. Although baptized a Catholic, she rarely went to church. For the next 40 years she held down a succession of menial jobs and earned enough simply to pay the rent on her council house home and keep herself in food. Her chief companions were her pet budgerigars.

Two years after becoming an old-age pensioner, Molly developed arthritis in her knees, had several falls which left her shaken and bruised and, after one such fall, was eventually admitted to hospital. There it was diagnosed that she also had cancer. It was in hospital that I first came across her and persuaded her to come to our monthly Masses for the sick.

After that she became a vital member of the parish, not because of her piety or her long suffering in the face of constant pain, but on account of her insistence on always speaking the truth. It was this quality which immediately established her as a friend of the children of the parish. They knew that, whatever they asked of Molly, she would never lie to them.

This quality took on a particular significance this month when not only the children but all of us at St Jude's were shaken by the cot death of a two-month-old baby called Katie. It was hard enough trying to comfort the parents of the baby and somehow make sense of the tragedy to the adult members of the parish, but how was I to explain such a death to the children? As it happened, Molly relieved me of the task.

Despite being so upset, the children from the school who provide the music for our Masses for the sick felt it was their duty to be present at Katie's funeral. Whereas they were accustomed to death occurring among the elderly, for most of them this was their first experience of a baby dying.

When I entered the church on the day of the funeral to make sure everything was in order, the children were there to rehearse the music. What initially puzzled me, however, was the way in which they were all sitting in great silence, looking towards the sanctuary, not fidgeting at all, but intent on listening to someone addressing them. Then I heard the voice of Molly.

Apparently she had arrived at the church early for the funeral and had gone to her usual pew to pray, where one of the children had found her. In next to no time, this same child had pulled her to her feet, thrust her walking frame into her hands and gently but persistently dragged her to the front of the church. There, in front of everyone, this same child had asked her why God had permitted Katie to die.

Without hesitating, Molly said that no one knew the answer to that. What she knew, however, was that Katie was now in heaven, a place where there was no pain or sickness and where Katie could now see Jesus face to face. She told the children that life was a journey and she asked them to remember the countless times they had said goodbye to people they loved setting out on journeys. That was what they were here for today, to say goodbye to Katie who had simply gone ahead of them on this journey. She emphasized that one day they would all see her again when they too reached heaven. We knew this, she said, because Jesus had promised it would be so that first Easter, 2,000 years ago.

After that the children's main concern was not Katie's death, since they believed Molly completely, but how she would fare in heaven without her mother to look after her. I am now seriously considering enrolling Molly as a catechist.

August

In which the pastor takes his holiday and sees how other parishes celebrate the liturgy.

I reached passport control. A round-faced woman looked up without frown or smile. She glanced at my photograph and then glanced at me. 'Why aren't you wearing your collar?' she asked.

Suppressing a discourteous reply, I answered, 'Because I am on holiday.'

'How can you be on holiday from being a priest?'

'I am not on holiday from being a priest, but I am on holiday.'

Then she smiled briefly, returned my passport, and allowed me to enter the country.

I called round to see my neighbour, Bill, the other day on my return and we laughed about the exchange. 'At the same time,' he added more seriously, 'it does illustrate the problem, doesn't it? Aren't holidays difficult for us?'

'Of course, it's good to be on holiday. Everyone needs a break,' Bill went on, 'and not everyone is as lucky as we are and able to take one. But there is often this complicated business of who we are and what we do;

identity and role become confused. That's what happened to you at passport control. That woman did not see you really as a person but as someone who did a job.'

I agreed with him, but then remarked that the distinction he was making was not clear-cut. Our work is not just work, a job, it is a vocation.

'Yes, but many others do vocational work, like doctors and nurses and teachers and social workers, yet they manage to have a break. They aren't ruled by their calling all the time.'

I agreed it was not simply a matter of vocation, or rather not only a matter of vocation. We pursued our discussion. I reflected: 'My sister, for example, felt a calling to be a teacher. That's her vocation. She trained and now she teaches. Being a teacher, if you like, is more than a job for her; it is an important part of who she is. But when she goes on holiday, she can leave being a teacher to one side. It's not just that there are no classes to be taught. Her being a teacher is not relevant. But it's not quite like that for you and me. We can't do that with priesthood. We may not have duties to perform; we can take a break from them; but we can't altogether leave priesthood aside. Who we are and what we are are linked inescapably. Now I come to think of it, I suppose that's what I meant when I told the woman at the passport counter I was not on holiday from being a priest, although I was on holiday.'

'And was it a good holiday?' Bill asked.

'It was very good,' I replied promptly, 'because I was staying with friends. I could relax. I could be off-duty.'

'Those holidays are the best,' Bill said. Then he asked, 'How was the liturgy?'

102

It was the natural next question. In many ways it illustrates neatly the situation for priests on holiday. We spend so much of our time celebrating liturgy, and then still go to church when we are away. We are glad to do it, but it sometimes seems to me like asking a doctor to call in and do an hour's surgery each week during his annual break.

There is, of course, one specific benefit from going to Mass on holiday. We have the chance to see the way others celebrate. It can be inspiring, so that we return with fresh ideas. It can also be a shock. It makes me examine my conscience. I have to ask myself whether I treat the parishioners at home in the same way.

Some years ago, on holiday in England, I visited two parishes during the fortnight I was away. I wondered how the people who went to Mass at these churches managed to attend regularly. I wondered whether I could have bothered had I been living locally. The preaching was dull and the singing thin.

The dull preaching was simply boring: predictable and unimaginative. I do not expect to remember the particular point of the sermons after such a period of time but I do remember how tedious they were. They were homilies preached for their own sake, which did not touch the heart. But I must ask myself, might not mine be the same?

The thin singing dragged. People presume that Catholics do not sing in church, and both these parishes confirmed that presumption. But it need not be so. I know parishes where the congregations sing with enthusiasm, including the one where I am stationed. There is a choir which leads the general singing, will sing in parts, and regularly extends its repertoire with good music. We may be lucky, but it is not really that difficult.

And to cap it all, the priests sadly lacked presidential skills: they seemed casual, apologetic, without presence. Again, I have to ask, do I seem like that?

These displays were as depressing as they were unnecessary. Our liturgy offers such scope for celebrating deeply and with dignity the mysteries of faith.

This year, to return to Bill's question, the liturgy was good. I return encouraged and revived.

September

In which the pastor reflects on ways of coping with requests for money.

A few years ago I received a postcard from a friend. It was a cartoon based on an old Irish proverb. It depicts a pious-looking, well-fed priest with his prayer book in one hand and waving a blessing with the other as he walks past a dishevelled and hungry-looking beggar. The caption underneath reads: 'A blessing doesn't fill the stomach.'

It is a message which continuously haunts me these days, because of the growing numbers of people whom I encounter begging on the streets. I always feel bad if I walk past someone begging without giving him or her at least some small change. And yet I know this is not always the most appropriate response.

When I was in the seminary we had an enlightened rector who invited a number of specialists and activists in the various fields to lecture us on the kind of social problems we would be likely to encounter in the course of our pastoral ministry.

I have always remembered a talk which was given by an Anglican priest who was deeply involved in a project for the single homeless. He warned us against being too ready to give 'hand-outs' which, he claimed, were just helping to keep people on the streets. This, I have no doubt, was more or less true in those days when the vast majority were either alcoholics or drug abusers, and there were sufficient places available in hostels for those who really wanted to be helped.

In recent years though, I fear, the situation has changed drastically. Many of those begging today look as if they are still in their teens. Many others look clearly disturbed and in need of daily supervision. On several occasions recently, when I have tried to find somewhere suitable for those genuinely seeking my help, I was simply unable to because of the lack of spaces that are available today or because of the complicated system of referrals that rules out anyone who doesn't fit easily into this or that category.

I have spent many frustrating hours on the telephone being referred from one group to another only to discover that none of the agencies seemed able or willing to help. Clearly once a person has reached the level of the streets it is very difficult to climb back into the system again. In such circumstances I have no hesitation in giving a person sufficient money to book into a bed and breakfast, in the hope that it gives him or her sufficient time to find a suitable alternative. Sadly, though, I frequently find the person back on the streets.

What adds to my frustration at my inability to deal with the problems of those in genuine need is the fact that the majority of those who call at our house seeking help are confidence tricksters. The other day a middle-aged man came to see me. He explained that he had been sleeping rough and that he needed his train fare so that he could visit a relative who was willing to help him but was living in another part of the country. He claimed that he had been to the local vicar who had chased him away and so I was his last resort.

I pointed out to him that I wasn't surprised at the vicar's reaction because his story didn't ring true. I told him that despite his unshaven face he didn't have the appearance of someone who slept in a doorway for several nights, as he was claiming. His silver-white hair was immaculately clean, his nails manicured, and the woollen track suit which he wore under a tattered old overcoat looked as if it had been put on fresh that morning. He immediately became abusive and then rushed to the door fearful no doubt that I might call the police if he didn't make a quick exit.

Over the years I have encountered so many similar situations that I have no doubt that there are a number of people like him who go from presbytery to vicarage, throughout the country, making a very good living from the hand-outs they receive. They carefully time themselves to arrive at the presbytery a few minutes before Mass, hoping no doubt that the priest will be under pressure and therefore more likely to give them something just in order to get rid of them. The tragedy is that not only are they using our limited resources, but also they are creating unnecessary pressures and distracting priests from focusing more time on those in genuine need.

The solution to this problem though is clearly within our own power, and the time for a crackdown on these confidence tricksters is long overdue. They will soon get fed up and stop pestering us if more priests refuse to be taken in so easily and stop giving hand-outs so readily.

The problem of the growing number of people on the streets, however, is well beyond our ability to cope and, in my opinion, calls for immediate political action. I suspect in the long run putting pressure on our local MP could be more effective than putting our hand in our pocket every time we are asked to do so.

October

In which the pastor faces a difficult decision and decides that love is not enough for a happy marriage.

Recently I received a telephone call from an anxious-sounding mother: 'My son wants to get married as soon as possible, when can he come to see you?'

My immediate reaction was to suspect that he must have made his girlfriend pregnant and was under pressure from the family to do what they saw to be the right thing. If that were so, I though to myself, I would advise them to wait until at least a year after the birth of the child. Otherwise I feared that they would never be sure whether they married because they really loved each other or because they felt they had to for the sake of the child and family respectability. Such outside pressures would call into question, of course, the validity of their consent which according to the rite of marriage should be given 'freely' and 'without reservation'.

When the couple arrived at the presbytery accompanied by his mother and some family friends, however, I found myself faced with a different kind of problem. Far from wanting to push them into marriage, both families had tried, but without success, to dissuade them because they considered them to be far too young. He was 19 and she only 16.

When I spoke to the couple on their own, I discovered that she was not, as I had feared, pregnant, and neither were they living together, even though they had run away from home a few weeks previously after her parents refused to give the consent required in such cases by civil law. It was clear to me that they were madly in love and I soon realized that there was no way in which I would be able to persuade them to wait a bit longer and not to rush into marriage. The uncomfortable question I had to face was, what should I do?

Even though I lack any personal experience of marriage I have been a priest long enough to know that for a successful marriage a couple need more than just to be in love. Over the years I have come to see compatibility as perhaps being even more important. This young couple had much in common. They were both from large families of travellers and had been brought up in a tradition which looks on marriage as a permanent commitment. I realized that their common upbringing would be helpful and enable them to understand each other better, though I still felt they were far too young to take on such a commitment as marriage. And yet I knew from talking to them that they were so intent on getting married that if I refused they would just look for someone else to conduct the ceremony. An added complication was the fact that we had just completed our parish pre-marriage preparation course and were not planning to hold another one for at least three months. They felt that they could not wait that long.

Rightly or wrongly I decided to go ahead with their marriage. They already had in their possession all the documents required by Church law, and I felt that despite their inexperience and my own misgivings I should respect the fact that they still had a basic human right to get married at that age. We met again on a couple of occasions as the Church law requires in order to talk through the Christian understanding of marriage and the obligations which they were accepting by getting married in the Church. On the day itself the couple were understandably a bit nervous but their wedding took place in great style.

A few days ago, however, I was sharing the dilemma I had had to face with a friend who felt very strongly that I had made the wrong decision. She had been allowed to get married three years ago, without proper preparation, by a kind old priest who thought he was making it easier for her and her non-Catholic partner by not insisting that they should take pre-marriage instruction. Within six months of being married she realized that she had made a serious mistake, and they have recently separated. In the light of this experience she felt that no one should be allowed to get married in the Church without giving at least one year's notice and being required to undergo a properly organized pre-marriage course.

In ideal circumstances I would fully agree. But in parish life, of course, circumstances are rarely ideal. Frequently I find myself faced with situations which require me to adapt my own way of thinking or even at times to compromise it. I believe this is the price any priest has to pay when he tries to exercise his ministry with a certain amount of compassion for the circumstances in which people find themselves. There are numerous times when either through pressure, inexperience, or just lack of awareness, I know I get things wrong. It is at times like this that I can only hope that the grace of God will in some way compensate for my own inadequacies

November

In which the pastor celebrates the centenary of St Jude's with a pop star and the press.

This month we at St Jude's celebrated the centenary of the consecration of the church. For several months prior to the day we had all planned or rehearsed a series of events to commemorate this milestone in the life of the parish. An exhibition of drawings, old photographs and cuttings from newspapers describing the church building and its history had been on display in the local library. A concert had been performed at our parish school. And the high point of the centenary celebrations was a Mass of thanksgiving. Just as the bishop of the time had been present to consecrate the church one hundred years ago, so our present father in God had come to be the chief concelebrant at our centenary Mass. This was to be followed by a buffet supper for all the parish provided by the ladies of the Union of Catholic Mothers in the church hall.

On paper every detail had been worked out and every eventuality had been anticipated, not least the presence among us on the day of the Lord Mayor and Lady Mayoress, our constituency MP, the local Anglican dean and leaders from the other churches, plus a variety of other civic dignitaries. Also among the VIPs, at the persistent request of the members of the parish youth club, we had included a former parishioner, now a famous pop star, who hitherto had only been called upon to open our bazaars or hand out prizes at our parish school.

Whenever I see this young man I am afraid I cannot help wondering why his appearance always causes such a fuss; to me he is still the rather cheeky schoolboy who preferred playing football to coming to Mass on Sundays. For the life of me, I simply do not appreciate what others find enjoyable in the kind of so-called music he sings to and strums on his guitar. Of course, what we had not reckoned on was the attention his attendance at our celebrations would attract from foreign journalists, in view of the tour he was about to make of the countries of the European Community.

On the evening in question the church was packed to capacity, the opening hymn was sung lustily and even the altar servers looked reasonably clean and tidy, with none of them for once either chewing gum or gazing at the roof and yawning. Everything proceeded according to plan until the bishop was at the lectern and half-way through his homily. It was at that point that I became aware of a noise emanating from the rear of the church. The next moment, with a red-faced sacristan in hot pursuit, there emerged from the sacristy a host of photographers and journalists all bent on reaching the top of the church, careless of the noise and interruption they were occasioning.

At first I thought they were anxious to interview the

bishop – I think he too fancied he was the object of their attentions – but the next moment, before anyone could so much as say 'Cheese', flash bulbs were popping and questions in broken English were being loudly hurled in the direction of our famous pop star. To give him his due, throughout these strange happenings he remained silent and dignified.

Our master of ceremonies had his own view of the matter. Within seconds he had enlisted the support of five Knights of St Columba, as well as the sacristan who had arrived at the scene puffing and panting from his run down the nave, and together they grabbed the intruders by the scruff of the neck and frog-marched them out of the building. As the invaders were being unceremoniously removed we heard them shouting a variety of epithets, mostly delivered, fortunately, in a mixture of foreign tongues and therefore not readily understood by the majority of the congregation. This did, however, enable the assembled throng to take pride in the fact that for once none of the trouble-makers was British.

After the Mass and during the buffet supper I thanked the pop star for his presence of mind, but found it more difficult to thank the MC. From the smug expression on his face I could not help wondering what precisely had happened to our foreign visitors once they had been ejected from the church and were out of sight of those of us inside. Though I had resented the noisy and rude interruption of our centenary celebrations and was grateful for the swift action taken, I hoped very much that no harm had come to our uninvited guests. I feared the worst, however, when I spotted the ugly black eye one of them

115

had given to our aged sacristan. When I attempted to commiserate with him, I received from him the assurance that our MC – a former sergeant-major in the Irish Guards – had given them in return considerably more than they had bargained for.

I am sorry to say that my assistant appeared to approve. We had surely just seen the Church militant in action, he quietly remarked. I had to remind him that it was meant to be the season of universal goodwill.

December

In which the pastor has a dream, and reflects on the importance of nativity plays.

I had a dream a couple of nights ago and for once I can remember it. I was at a carol service and the church, which I did not recognize, but which was large and old, was packed with rugger hearties. They were singing lustily and without thought, 'O come, O come, Emmanuel', when suddenly the doors at the far end were flung wide and their prayer was answered. The Lord strolled down the aisle, looking about him in a rather matter-of-fact way, as the singing faded and jaws fell slack. I woke up laughing.

This happy dream caught my mood of the last few weeks. Advent is my favourite season. And the buzz about the parish has been a delight.

The mood, however, was disturbed by Geoff. He is a parishioner who is deputy head of a Catholic primary school about 15 miles away. I have never visited it, but it has a good reputation, especially for the way it deals with the depressed social conditions of the area. His problem is the new parish priest, appointed in the summer, who has forbidden them to have a Nativity play.

'What can I say to him?' Geoff implored me. 'We've

always had a Nativity play. It's the highlight of our end of term celebrations. Give me some good theological arguments I can use against him.'

Let me say at once that my sympathies lie entirely with Geoff, but good theological arguments tend not to spring to my mind on demand. So I asked what reasons this priest had given for his edict.

'Oh, he gives any number of reasons,' Geoff replied. 'He says that Advent is such a rich season, but so short, we should take full advantage of it. He argues that it is meant to be a time of preparation for Christmas, and so we shouldn't anticipate the feast. To do so makes a nonsense of Advent. And he says that, if we do anticipate it, we spoil it for the children, because we make its actual celebration an anticlimax.'

They were the reasons I had expected, the arguments of well-intentioned purists that I had heard before. I was no more impressed than Geoff. We talked for a while. It occurred to us both that what was needed was not theology, but a little common sense. It is not as though a Nativity play were Christmas itself.

In my experience, to hold a Nativity play at the end of term, a few days before the great feast, far from detracting from Advent, draws its preparatory work to its natural conclusion. By all means, avoid singing, 'Born this happy morning', if you wish, but I have never known a child find Christmas an anticlimax because of a Nativity play in school. On the contrary, a well-prepared play can be an invaluable way of helping the young grow in their awareness of what the birth of Jesus means.

The play in our own primary school this year has been

118

great fun and illustrates the point. I have managed to catch a couple of rehearsals as well as the main performance.

The plot is simplicity itself. Angels appear to shepherds and offer to show them something special, but a small angel gets separated from the others and left behind. We follow her as she goes off on her own in search of what is special. She finds beautiful snow, lovely decorations, exciting toys and tables groaning under scrumptious food, but none of these, she realizes, is the special sight promised to the shepherds. Then she sees a star shining brightly, follows it, and comes to the stable and the new-born babe.

This brief outline cannot capture either the atmosphere in the performance or the power of the lesson. With the help of music and laughter we delighted in the good things, but learnt not to allow them to distract us from the great fact at the heart of Christmas, the birth of a child who is one of us, but also truly God.

How anyone can imagine that preparing and performing such a play is in conflict with the spirit of Advent and impairs the celebration of Christmas is beyond me. Rather, it fulfils the very purpose of the season by preparing the young for Christmas. We certainly had an evening to remember. Children and teachers, parents and parishioners came together in joyous celebration. And there is another point. For some it will sadly be the closest they will come to any celebration of Christmas at all. Who would want to deny them even this? For others, however, it will gladly be a taste of the fuller celebration that follows.

And for those who may still want a theological reason

to confound the purists, I offer the one I learnt from that admirable Jesuit theologian and preacher, Walter Burghardt: at this feast, Christ himself is the greatest gift; and he does not come in a package marked, 'Not to be opened before Christmas'; Christmas is every day – if you prepare the way.

'O come, O come, Emmanuel.' Come now.

January

In which the parish loses its *beadsman* and
the pastor receives a visit from the police.

In the parish we are suffering a sense of loss and
loneliness, and it seems impossible to pray or talk about
anything else. You must excuse our tendency to be
inward-looking, but we are, after all, a family and we have
had to face a severe loss which none of us expected or
thought possible. Why should the tragedy of a solitary and
lonely man affect us so deeply?

Let me explain and in the process perhaps exorcise
some of the pain. Every parish should have a *beadsman*
who is expected to call down God's blessing in return for
our alms. Our *beadsman* was part of the family, he was
known to all, and like the black sheep he was often a
confounded nuisance.

His name was Locke, and he would never admit to a
Christian name. That he was Irish, his very speech
betrayed him; that he was frequently less than sober was
underlined by his unsteady gait and the bottle (usually of
a kind of paint-stripping wine) hanging dangerously from
his coat pocket. Yet if you put a spade in his hand you
were faced by a man in his element. The broad shoulders,

the way he spat on his hard hands, the switch and cut of the spade into the earth, all spoke of the craftsman at work. He could earn a living anywhere, and did.

Now the gardeners in the parish had warned me that three conifers planted in the school grounds were too close to the church wall. Locke asked for a fork, a wheelbarrow, and a spade (and a fiver) and set to work. By the end of the morning all three conifers were replanted. One of them, however, had failed to survive replanting, and stood there brown and dying: it would have to go.

Today as I draw up the rotas of altar servers and make out the notices of times of Confessions and Masses, I can see that dying conifer for whose removal and incineration our *beadsman* demanded another fiver and I refused, telling him that he could not expect to be paid for work ill-done. And I miss him now that he is dead like that third tree he planted.

Yesterday, the police called. They seemed so big in our small waiting-room, with their bleeping radios breaking through our conversation with incomprehensible messages concerning the identification of a body found on the line some distance down from our local railway station. They showed me a photograph of one side of a head; the other side was unrecognizable. Did I know him? I could not be sure. Would I get into the car and come with them to see?

We arrived at the mortuary. It was Locke all right, and may the Lord have mercy on his soul. The white tiled walls echoed our call to Our Father in heaven, and one of the constables, being a Catholic, joined in the Hail Mary.

On a table at the side were the dead man's clothes and possessions, prominent among them the black overcoat I had given him with its frayed collar and sagging pockets, stained with blood where the bottle had broken. My memories of that coat and its travels were now inextricably linked with that dead and twisted body. Lord have mercy on him.

On the table was a bloodstained envelope which the officer assured me was addressed to the church. I opened it and inside there were 33 £10 notes and a fiver together with a bill for £340 for repairs to the Community Centre. Locke had indeed done the repairs but I had not yet paid him for the work because I had not received his bill. The police suspected that the money had been stolen. I do not believe it. He had saved it, I think, and wanted to surprise us. When the train struck him as he staggered on the track, well over the limits of alcohol tolerance, he had still been short of the £340 by just £5. And I had refused him that last fiver for the removal of the dead tree.

Why did Locke have to wander lonely along that railway line? All around us we have council property which has passed into the hands of private ownership. What has become of the millions in purchase prices they saved? Where are the homes of the homeless?

We shall give the Midnight Mass collection, as is our wont, to some agreed charity. This year, in pain and shame and loss, we shall send the money to a housing aid society. May the Christ Child and his mother and St Joseph, lonely and abandoned in their stable, have us all in their keeping.

February

In which the bishop calls a meeting and the pastor reflects on the importance of parish visiting.

The bishop has been asking deaneries to gather in pairs during Lent to meet him. It is an opportunity for us all to exchange views, express our concerns and encourage one another. It has proved to be a welcome and useful exercise. But during his remarks when he was with us, the bishop said something which took me aback.

'Father,' he observed, 'I am sure I don't need to impress upon you the importance of visiting parishioners regularly in their own homes.'

'Hello,' I thought to myself, 'I've entered a time-warp.'

The point he was making, of course, is beyond dispute: there is no substitute for knowing personally the men, women and children we have been called to serve. But the means invoked – regular home visits – comes from a different age. It is out of touch with the reality we face.

When I first came to this parish, it was midsummer. I had hoped to do some visiting in those early months before the schools reopened in September. It was an ideal opportunity. It never happened. Even then time was squeezed by particular demands. Yet the bishop is right: personal contact is vital. His remarks set me thinking.

It dawned on me that I visit in fact more homes than I was at first aware. The character of the visiting may have changed; it is no longer the kind of systematic trawl, street by street, recommended by the bishop which I used to do many years ago, when I was first ordained; none the less, I am still out regularly.

There are happy occasions, social events in which I am included, and sad occasions, calls from those in need. It may be a family crisis. Or someone may have died. All priests are familiar with those calls from undertakers with the news of a parishioner's death when the name is as unknown to us as the inside of a church is to the departed – and often to their relatives as well. Still, I always visit if I possibly can. It is a delicate time. You can never be sure how the family will react. People shrouded in grief can be numb or angry. But I find they usually thank me for calling and often add: 'I didn't think you'd bother.' Then I feel well rewarded.

I also visit regularly those who are sick or housebound. This parish is large. Eucharistic ministers make these visits most frequently, as they should, but I do not want to lose contact with the sick altogether. So I have divided the parish into districts and go round each one month by month on the first Friday. In this way I see them all at least twice a year. It can be an effort to go out, but once again I am often rewarded, sometimes by humour, sometimes by inspiration, and sometimes by gratitude.

Ronnie has only just moved into the parish. He is

in a residential home. He is blind, well into his seventies, and perhaps a little simple. I was called out to see him.

'Here's Father, Ronnie,' the nurse said. He turned towards the sound of her voice. His sightless eyes gazed about him and he stretched out a hand to shake mine firmly.

'Hello,' he said, then asked at once, 'shall I give you a song?'

The nurse, who was leaving, swivelled on her heel, her face a composition of alarm, alertness and humour. 'Keep it clean, Ron,' she cautioned.

Without more ado he burst into a full-voiced rendering of 'Mammy'. At the end, he let out a gale of laughter and announced, 'Ah'm a frisky fellow, me,' and laughed again. So did the nurse. So did I.

Later that morning I called on Mrs McGarry. She is very old and sometimes confused, but not on this occasion. Midway through the 'Our Father', she broke off to comment: 'Isn't it a wonderful prayer, Father? It has everything in it, everything you could possibly want to say.'

I agreed with her automatically, we finished the prayer, I gave her Communion, and shortly afterwards I left. Then, a few days later, her words came back to me. They detonated in my mind. The comprehensiveness of the prayer struck me as never before. Since then it has been a little difficult to say it in public, because I want to go very slowly. I want to ponder its power and drink in its phrases: 'Thy kingdom come'; 'Thy will be done'; 'Give us this day our daily bread'; 'Forgive us our trespasses'.

Then there's Gerald. He returned to the Church two years ago, when his wife died. For a while he used to walk to Mass on Sundays, but now ill-health has limited his movements. As I was leaving him recently, he took me by surprise, 'Thank you, Father,' he said, 'for all you have done for me.' And then he went on simply and naturally: 'I pray for you every night and thank God for you every morning, when I wake.'

I was lost for words. Here it was evident that out of sight did not mean out of mind. The style of visiting may have altered, but its value remains. I receive Christ from Gerald as surely as he receives the Eucharist from me. And I give thanks.

March

In which the pastor discovers that enthusiasm for Christian unity is on the wane.

An 87-year-old parishioner who has great difficulty in walking and has been waiting for several months to have a hip replacement, finally received notification that her operation is scheduled for the end of the month. The letter from the hospital advised her not to bring too many personal belongings. It did, however, recommend that she should bring a tracksuit. Obviously her surgeon is confident in his ability to work wonders.

I only wish I could have the same sense of confidence about the future ecumenical movement which, despite the Pope's efforts to encourage progress, seems to be limping to a halt.

I live in an area which has a good reputation for ecumenical activity. Ten years ago, you could have guaranteed that there would have been standing room only at the annual ecumenical service in the Week of Prayer for Christian Unity. This year, however, our local Anglican church was over two-thirds empty and the majority of those present were well into what could be described as their twilight years. They were the old faithfuls who had carried the torch for unity right from the early days of the ecumenical movement.

The absence of young single people and families was noticeable. I have no means of knowing whether this phenomenon is peculiar to my area or whether it reflects a trend in the country as a whole. I suspect it may be the latter. Certainly I know a number of young singles and couples who faithfully attend Mass every Sunday but have no interest whatsoever in getting involved in any institutional structures of the church.

Our local Anglican and Methodist ministers tell me that the younger members of their congregations show a similar reluctance. Like their Catholic contemporaries, they are quite happy to attend worship but shy away when it comes to taking on further responsibility and getting involved in parish activities.

It is not that they are selfish or lack interest in church life. Family commitments and the pressure of work are the most obvious reasons why some of our young members find it impossible to take on further responsibilities. There are also the peer-group pressures they face. The fact that they go to Mass regularly already marks them out as somewhat peculiar to many of their secular friends and associates. For them to become actively involved in parish life would undoubtedly isolate them still further. 'He's got religion' tends to be regarded as a derogatory tag at every level of society in Britain today.

Besides all this there is, I fear, an even more serious obstacle. Many of my younger friends who are deeply spiritual have nevertheless expressed an anxiety about becoming too involved in the life of the parish as a community because of what they see as its restrictive and, at times, petty nature.

I can fully understand and sympathize with their reluctance. Sadly, not everyone who gets actively involved in parish community life does so for purely altruistic motives. People frequently bring their own agenda. The consequence is that they frighten away those who simply want to give their time and talents in the service of others.

The internal state of community life in the mainstream Churches is undoubtedly reflected in the ecumenical movement. The notable absence of young people on such occasions as the annual unity service should sound a warning note in the minds of all our church leaders.

The majority of young people, married or single, who come to church, in my experience, are seeking the spiritual sustenance that will enable them to cope with the pressures and the unpredictable nature of their secular lives. They are not interested in getting caught up in internal squabbles or the polemics of inter-Church life.

I have been gradually aware that a number of young people from various denominational backgrounds attend Mass regularly at our parish. They are not interested in any kind of formal reception into the Catholic Church, for they feel no need to abandon their own family tradition. They come to us, they say, because they feel spiritually at home.

They are what I would call the new breed of ecumenists. Here are the people we should be listening to if we want to put new life, direction and step into a movement that seems to be running out of steam.

April

**In which the pastor overhears a hurtful remark
and takes four funerals.**

One of the refrains throughout my years as a priest has been to pray for peace, 'especially in Northern Ireland'. A peace process was under way at last there – but was suddenly thrown into confusion, if not perhaps actual jeopardy, by events set in train by a paedophile priest.

I was in Marks and Spencer's the other day, my collar obscured by my scarf. I had gone to buy a sweater. As I searched, I inadvertently overheard one woman say to another: 'Catholic priests? I wouldn't trust them. All they do is abuse children.'

I felt stunned, too shocked to protest. The sweeping judgment stung, in spite of its injustice. The sting was supplied by the element of truth. I felt ashamed.

Yet I know there are so many priests who seek to develop an interior life, who are faithful in prayer, who spend themselves with unsung generosity in the service of those entrusted to their care, whose commitment to celibacy is unblemished and capacity for friendship undiminished, and who cope cheerfully with the range of expectations laid upon them.

I do not want to make special claims for this parish, nor certainly for myself. We are quite ordinary. But even a partial snapshot of this week may be revealing. As well as all the regular tasks to be done, it has been a case, not so much of Four Weddings and a Funeral, as Four Funerals and a Celebration.

The first funeral was a Requiem Mass one evening for Vittorio. He died in Italy, but two of his sons live in the parish with their families and there was a large gathering of the local Italian community to commend him to God and give thanks for his life. I had never met him. He has been too old to visit his family since I came to the parish, but they have regularly visited him. When he became seriously ill a fortnight ago and died, they were not able to return in time for his funeral. It was important to say Mass for him and try to comfort them.

The next day Maureen was buried. She had been virtually bed-ridden for years, looked after heroically by her husband, a prickly man whom I much admire. He has as much right to be prickly as she in her circumstances to be awkward and demanding. His own health has not been good, for he has been a prey to shingles. He shuffled into Mass this morning. In a way, Maureen's death can be seen as a blessed release for them both, but I suspect it will not be so simple. I must keep an eye on him.

Maurice, who was in his early seventies, was found dead in bed on Tuesday morning. He lived with his widowed sister. He had read at Mass last Sunday, with a firm clear voice. He has been a respected member of the parish throughout his life, always ready to lend an unobtrusive hand, whenever it was needed, and he will be greatly missed by many of us. His reading ended: 'Grace and mercy await those he has chosen.' We shall commend him to the Lord on Monday, mourning our loss, but with special confidence.

And, finally, there is Thomas who also is not known to me personally, long lapsed from the Church and not living in this parish. His daughter, who comes here regularly, called to see me as his condition deteriorated, to tell me she thought he would now be ready to receive a priest again. 'What shall I do?' she asked. 'Will you come?'

I thought it better that she contact his own parish priest, which she did and most happily. Now Thomas has died and she has asked to have the funeral here. The local priest has agreed and we have made the arrangements for Tuesday.

As for the celebration, well, that is not quite accurate. It was rather a meeting about celebration. Our diocesan Ministry to Priests Team had planned an in-service day on preparing the liturgy. It went well.

Some people will turn up for anything, but there were characters there that you do not always see and it was an encouragement to find brother priests, still full of enthusiasm, searching for ways to make the liturgy come alive. We shared experience of liturgies past, good practice and bad, studied key scriptural passages, and reflected on the seasons' symbols. Nor did we do this alone. We had been asked to bring a parish catechist along with us, if possible. Their presence and experience heightened immeasurably the value of the day. It was good, as priests and people, to be working together.

There is much devotion, indeed, in priesthood. We

know, however, that there are times when we fail as priests, and our failures are the more serious because they often damage others. 'The only prayer I ever offer for myself is for fidelity,' a priest friend of mine told me recently. Many of us pray that prayer and we ask others to pray it with us.

May

In which the pastor deals with demanding visitors and wonders if he is wise to hand out cash.

On the first Saturday of the month, I was looking forward to a quiet day. There were to be some confessions and the vigil Mass, but otherwise I had no appointments. When my alarm went off, I turned over and went back to sleep. I got up shortly after half-past eight.

The doorbell rang as I was climbing out of the bath. I was expecting the postman with a parcel, so I wrapped a towel round me, stuck my head through the bedroom window, and called out. But it was not the postman.

The woman who had rung my bell had called before. She alleges she is victimized by her neighbours, lives under constant threat of sexual assault from men who loiter on the pavement opposite her house, and is regularly assaulted physically by the police when she goes to complain. These matters afflict her in her mind. They are no less real for her on that account; perhaps they are more real; but it is not easy to bring her the help she needs.

She had heard me call out and kept ringing the bell. I

dressed as quickly as possible and went down to the front door. We had talked before at length on a number of occasions, and I felt this was not the time for a long meeting. She wanted me to come with her to confront the neighbours who, she said, were noisy and beating on her windows and nearly breaking them. It was typical that no window had in fact been broken. Although I have been to her home several times and, indeed, accompanied her to the police station, I decided on this occasion I would not go back with her.

When she realized I would not do as she asked, she turned sharply and was gone. I watched her go. I have no doubt she will be back.

It is not easy to know how best to help her. She dismisses at once any suggestion that she might see a doctor, but I am sure that is the real help she needs at present. I try to treat her with seriousness and respect, but I feel I must not be drawn into inhabiting her world. Simply to do as she wished would not, I judged, have been helpful. But was I right?

The rest of the morning was uneventful.

In the afternoon I said a prayer as I sat down. The prayer was for a quiet afternoon. I was sitting in front of the television watching a match. Was it prudence or too little faith that prompted me to switch on the video recorder as well? I do not know. But my prayer was not answered. Within minutes, the doorbell rang.

Standing in the porch was a sad-looking woman in her thirties whom I had never seen before. It was soon plain that the meeting was going to take some time, partly because she could not speak coherently. I thought at first she had an impediment, but soon realized it was more a nervous condition which made it very hard for her to put her words together intelligibly.

Her story emerged slowly and unclearly. Though her situation was not extreme, it was very difficult and she needed a fair sum of money, though not a vast sum. She seemed helpless, rather lost and inadequate. At one stage, she admired the presbytery and wondered how many others had lived there. It is a large house where I live alone. And she suddenly asked whether God loved her, even though she was poor, 'or does he just love those who are rich and live in big houses?' She spoke without guile.

There were questions I needed to ask her as well. I asked some of them, but felt inhibited by her anxiety and embarrassment. Was this an elaborate con? I have been conned in the past, but, like so many priests, I fear refusing the genuinely needy.

I gave her the money she asked for, my own, not the parish's, and she left. She needed a mark of confidence and respect.

Did I treat these two women wisely? Should I have been more forthcoming in the morning and rather tougher in the afternoon? I am not sure.

It left me thinking about the way we can speak readily about Christ's identification with the poor and the marginalized, but how do we discern Christ in the mentally unstable and the socially inept? He can be well disguised there. At least by showing respect we acknowledge his presence.

June

In which the pastor praises the sacristan and laments the fact that elderly people are insufficiently valued.

Our parish sacristan is a remarkable man. Now in his late eighties, he has served the Church in this voluntary role since his retirement from work more than 20 years ago. Every morning he arrives early to open the church and to prepare the altar for Mass. If I, or my assistant, should fail to appear in the sacristy in good time, he will make his way into our house, rap on one of our bedroom doors and ask in a loud voice: 'Are you up, Father?'

He left school at the age of 14 and had to work hard with his hands all his life. He is the sort of person who immediately shies away from any kind of formal discussion group, and yet he has a most profound grasp of the Christian faith which he articulates with ease whenever the need arises. The other day, preparing for a funeral, we began to discuss the importance of the corporal works of mercy in the life of the Christian. He repeated to me, without the slightest hesitation, the complete list of these charitable virtues. He told me that he had learnt them from the catechism as a boy at school and had always regarded them as important points of reference in his relationship with God and others.

He is just one of a number of elderly people who are a great help and support in the daily life of the parish. They are involved in administration, typing, counting the weekly collections, visiting their neighbours, washing the church linen, answering the presbytery telephone and door and, perhaps most important of all, praying every day for the well-being of the parish team and community.

They belong to a generation that I have come greatly to admire. Having lived through a world war (sometimes two), they have a real sense of what is and what is not important. All of them seem to have a good grasp of the essentials of Christian faith, combined with a deep understanding of what parish community is all about. Once they have committed themselves to doing something, I have always found them to be totally reliable and utterly dependable. If, through illness or absence from the parish, they are unable to fulfil their duties, they usually arrange for a suitable replacement in good time and do not expect me or the parish secretary to make alternative arrangements at the last minute.

Their loyalty and sense of duty, though, is firmly rooted in the person of Christ. So their service and commitment to the life of the parish does not depend upon whether they like or dislike the personality of the parish priest. on the few occasions that I have had reason to have cross words with our sacristan, he has reminded me politely that what he does is for God and not to please me.

I am certain that people like these are to be found in

every parish in the world. Too often, however, elderly people are regarded only as in need of care and attention. Even in a parish, their potential can easily be overlooked if we get locked within the sort of mentality that is common these days and that looks on age as some sort of social handicap in itself. They have the experience of life, the talent, the professionalism and, equally important, the time to get involved and to do things properly.

The Church should show, especially at the level of our parish communities, how the elderly can become actively involved. Even those who are housebound, I have found, can make a worthwhile contribution to the overall life of the parish, provided we resist that natural temptation to write them off simply because of their lack of mobility.

Someone who has difficulty in walking has not lost the ability to type or to write letters in order to raise funds for charitable causes. Elderly people can also be a powerhouse of prayer, interceding for the needs not only of the parish community, but of our divided and poverty-stricken world. I have felt reassured and strengthened in my pastoral work by my knowledge that a number of our elderly parishioners pray daily for me, and for those to whom I minister.

I have become conscious of how much we depend upon this older generation to maintain our present parochial structures. I suspect many other parish priests may feel the same. This makes me wonder what will happen to the present parish system once they have passed on to their well deserved heavenly reward.

July – and *Envoi*

In which the pastor bids farewell to St Jude's.

Approximately twice a year there occur in our diocese what my assistant describes facetiously as the episcopal spring and autumn manoeuvres. By this he means those occasions when the bishop moves certain priests from one parish to another or from one assignment to another. For some of us, then, the months before spring and autumn tend to be anxious times.

This month has been one of those times. After all, the appointment of clergy is usually one of the most sensitive issues in the life of any diocese. It raises such questions as the criteria by which changes are made, how a bishop informs or persuades a priest that it is time he moved, how long a priest should remain in a particular parish or line of work, and what provision is or should be made for his eventual retirement. The whole area is a mine-field.

Clergy not keen to move have been trying to keep a low profile this month, offering profuse apologies for their absence from meetings where they might bump into the bishop. This was not a time to remind him of their existence or of the complaints he might have received from some of their disgruntled parishioners.

For virtually all the clergy, imminent spring or autumn moves are matters of immense speculation, lengthy telephone calls to one another, endless debate on the golf course and even occasions for a mild flutter. When processing into church recently at a newly ordained priest's first Mass, I was amazed at the speed with which a priest behind me was rattling off for the benefit of his neighbour all the rumours he had heard about forthcoming redeployments. I felt quite unnerved.

For some priests, however, the possibility of change is a desirable prospect, a challenge, or even a source of welcome relief. Among assistant priests there is often considerable debate about who is the 'Head Waiter' – next in line by seniority for a parish.

My assistant has been in the habit of telling me how different is the procedure followed in more than a few North American dioceses. In these, apparently, when a parish falls vacant for such reasons as the death or retirement of the parish priest, the vacancy is advertised in the diocesan newspaper and any priest in the diocese may apply to become the new pastor. A personnel board, made up of representatives of the bishop, priests and people, visits the parish in question and, after examining the parish plant, speaking with the parish council and listening to different parishioners and so on, draws up a profile of its needs. The personal profiles of priests who have applied for the post are then put alongside that of the parish and the one who seems to come closest to fulfilling the parish's needs is interviewed and usually given the job. If two priests have more or less identical qualifications, only then is the senior by ordination given the parish.

I have gradually realized that nothing will convince him that the American system is not foolproof and not necessarily better than the system of appointments made by our bishop. This does not prevent him becoming immensely intrigued by the latter method. Twice a year he develops enthusiasm for gossip about clergy moves akin to that of a trainspotter collecting number plates.

When therefore a letter arrived for me this month from the bishop's residence, bearing on the envelope his distinctive coat of arms depicting a sprig of holly at its centre, addressed in his own hand, and obviously containing important news, my assistant was agog. I must confess that I deliberately let the letter lie unopened on the table in the presbytery hall for an unusually long time, indeed a whole morning, simply to whet his appetite and stimulate his imagination. I knew, of course, what it contained. The bishop had telephoned me several weeks previously asking if I would care to leave St Jude's in the autumn and take up a new appointment in a different diocese.

After lunch on the day the letter arrived, I felt it would be cruel to keep my assistant in suspense any longer and opened the letter in front of him. I must admit to satisfaction when I observed the transfixed expression on his face and his open-mouthed impatience to hear my news. But when I quietly informed him of the letter's contents and added that I would be taking up the bishop's suggestion and leaving St Jude's in two months' time, he

146

did not bat an eyelid. Instead, he amazed me by calmly announcing that he had changed his mind completely about our diocesan system of appointments. Apparently he now considered it an excellent method of assigning priests to different parishes or tasks.

Only later did it occur to me that my assistant is the current Head Waiter.

Subject Index

If you have enjoyed this book, you may like to know that Pastor Ignotus continues to observe the parish scene through his regular column in THE TABLET.

To join him and a team of other first-class writers in their exploration of religion, politics, current affairs and the arts, let us send you a complimentary copy of the paper for three weeks.

Write to Tablet Enterprises, FREEPOST, London W6 0BR.

Telephone: 0181 748 8484

http://www.thetablet.co.uk

THE
TABLET
the international Catholic weekly